VOICES FROM FATHERHOOD

Fathers, Sons, and ADHD

PATRICK J. KILCARR, Ph.D.

PATRICIA O. QUINN, M.D.

BRUNNER/MAZEL, *Publishers* · NEW YORK
A member of the Taylor & Francis Group

Library of Congress Cataloging-in-Publication Data

Kilcarr, Patrick J.
    Voices from fatherhood : fathers, sons, and ADHD / Patrick J.
Kilcarr, Patricia O. Quinn.
        p.   cm.
    Includes bibliographical references
    ISBN 0-87630-858-2
    1. Attention-deficit-disordered children—Family relationships.
2. Fathers and sons. 3. Attention-deficit disordered youth—Family
relationships.   I. Quinn, Patricia O.   II. Title.
RJ506.H9K55 1997
618.92'8589—dc21   97-129
                                                                                         CIP

Cover design by Brigid McCarthy
Illustrations by Brendan Beyrer

Published by
Brunner/Mazel, Inc.
A member of the Taylor & Francis Group
1900 Frost Rd. Suite 101
Bristol, PA 19007

Manufactured in the United States of America

10 9 8 7 6 5 4 3 2 1

To my loving wife, Donna, who has never let go of the rope; to my sons, Payton, Bryce, Mason, Trent, and Troy, who define the meaning of life; to my father, who never stopped believing in me; and to my mother, who encouraged me to believe in myself.

P.J.K.

To my husband, Joe, who has supported me in all of my endeavors for all of these years and has been a caring, loving father to our four children.

P.O.Q.

ACKNOWLEDGMENTS

We would like to extend our deep gratitude to all of those who supported us throughout this project. Especially:

Those fathers who participated in this book and recognized the importance of sharing their story with other fathers.

Rob Truhn who put in countless hours reviewing the manuscript.

Ellen McHugh for her tireless transcriptions of the interview tapes.

Wade Horn for his valuable feedback regarding this work.

Susan Kent Cakars for her editorial expertise.

While the stories contained in this book come from interviews with fathers of sons with ADHD, names and ages have been changed to maintain confidentiality and anonymity.

TABLE OF CONTENTS

◆ ◆ ◆

Preface for Fathers ix

Wisdom's Path xi

Introduction: Life's Journey xiii

Chapter 1   What ADHD Is and Isn't 1

How ADHD Affects . . .

Chapter 2   Parenting 17

Chapter 3   Fatherhood 28

Chapter 4   Families 55

Managing ADHD . . .

Chapter 5   Discipline 77

Chapter 6   Behavior Management Strategies 92

Chapter 7   Medication Issues 110

Living with ADHD . . .

Chapter 8   Surviving Adolescence 126

Chapter 9   Sons Grown to Men 141

Chapter 10   Conclusion 164

Epilogue: Voices from Grandfatherhood 171

Resources 178

PREFACE FOR FATHERS

◆ ◆ ◆

Writing this book marks in many ways the beginning of my journey as a father of two sons with ADHD. Through the years I have learned a great deal about ADHD. However, it was while interviewing the fathers you will hear from in this book that I realized how much more I have to learn, as well as to share. I am reminded of the time many years ago when I was a trainee in an outdoor adventure program. We were learning to lead young adolescents in a variety of outdoor adventure activities, the most challenging of which was backcountry wilderness travel. When I first applied to the apprenticeship program, I had a limited understanding of the enormous responsibility that awaited me.

The training program spanned several months, challenging me in every conceivable way: emotionally, physically, behaviorally, and spiritually. One evening, as I sat out under the stars, one of the instructors asked if I felt ready to lead a trip alone with another instructor. Up to that point, I had never had direct responsibility for the safety and emotional well-being of the participants. I recall feeling a shudder of fear, and then saying, "Well, I have learned a lot, but there is so much more for me to learn. I don't know if I could solve all the problems that will come up on a trip."

My instructor, who was also like a mentor to me, said, "You know you are ready to lead when you realize there is so much more to learn. Establishing a relationship with the outdoors and the people you lead is a process, not an event. It is more than knowing a bunch of skills; it is knowing how and when to use them, and when to let the group or individual you are leading struggle themselves to find a solution. Even though they may have a hard time and get frustrated, you stand by them—acknowledging their strength, creativity, and ability."

This is precisely the challenge that we face as fathers of sons who have ADHD. As Alexandre Dumas wrote, "One's work may be finished someday, but one's education never." We can never have enough understanding, compassion, and knowledge to support our sons as they learn how to adequately cope with their ADHD.

Patrick J. Kilcarr

Over the twenty-five years that I have dealt with children with ADHD, I have repeatedly been filled with a sense of awe and appreciation for their parents. Those fathers and mothers sincerely searching for answers and yet filled with the hope that they can make a difference and help their sons and daughters achieve success and happiness in this world. They unselfishly sacrifice, wanting to do what is best for their children. Often they wish to spare their children the pain, hurt, and humiliation they suffered growing up in a world where people did not understand disabilities, a world where they were perceived as being dumb or lazy.

Fathers particularly have touched me with their wit and wisdom. They seem to be able to get at what is important and have a sense of what needs to be done. In talking with these men over the years, I have found that they earnestly sought answers and solutions and readily acknowledged when they were wrong. They didn't always do so easily, however, and needed to be given the opportunity to discuss their concerns and feelings. It is my hope that this book will provide an opening for that discussion.

Patricia O. Quinn

WISDOM'S PATH

My mother was a good woman. I thought she was the wisest person in the whole world. So one day—when I was just a little feller, maybe six or seven—I asked her how I could become wise like her. She just laughed and said I was awfully young to be asking such questions. But, she said, since I asked, she would tell me. "Life is like a path"; she said, smiling down at me, "and we all have to walk the path. If we lay down, we even lay down on that path. If we live through the night, we have to get up and start walking down that path again. As we walk down that path we'll find experiences like little scraps of paper in front of us along the way. We must pick up those pieces of scrap paper and put them in our pockets. Every single scrap of paper we come to should be put into that pocket. Then, one day, we will have enough scraps of paper to put together and see what they say. Maybe we'll have enough to make some sense. Read the information and take it to heart. Then put the pieces back in that pocket and go on, because there will be more pieces to pick up. Later we can pull them out and study them and maybe learn a little more. If we do this all through life, we'll know when to pull out those scraps to read more of the message. The more we read, the more we'll learn the meaning of life. We can become wise, or at least wiser than we were."

Uncle Frank Davis—Pawnee, *Wisdom Keepers,* pp. 100–101

Published with permission from the book *Wisdom Keepers* © 1990 Steve Wall and Harvey Arden; Beyond Words Publishing, Inc., 4443 NE Airport Road, Hillsboro, OR 97124; 800-284-9673.

INTRODUCTION

LIFE'S JOURNEY

Whenever we plan a journey, there are preparations that can be made in advance to assure that things will run smoothly. These include obtaining information about the country or region we plan to visit, checking the climate, studying the language spoken there, becoming more knowledgeable about the inhabitants, and deciding on a final destination. These guiding principles also apply when we face life's journey with our children who have ADHD.

We need factual information about ADHD and knowledge of the emotional climate of both our children and ourselves. We need to understand the language of our children and interpret the jargon of the professionals who care for them. The inhabitants of this world who have ADHD are unique and complex individuals whose strengths can far outshine their weaknesses if given the proper encouragement and the belief that they are loved and cherished. Living with children with extreme hyperactivity may feel like being caught in the middle of a firestorm. If a parent also has ADHD, there may be additional turbulence due to the emotional drama that often unfolds between the parent and the child. Individuals with ADHD are perceptive and sensitive, and experience intense emotions. Without a reliable map and compass, it can be easy to lose our way in the storms that arise due to ADHD.

The powerful description that begins this book, "Wisdom's Path," reminds us that our journey in life requires walking down many paths. Sometimes we travel alone, other times with someone else. Our experiences are the scraps of paper found along the way. It is our intention in this book to share with you information to "put into your pocket." Fathers who are traveling the same journey share their experiences and encouragement. These scraps of information, when pieced together, hold the power to help you create the strongest possible relationship with your child.

As the father of a child with ADHD you probably have many questions about the characteristics of ADHD and their effect on your child. Often fathers do not get their questions answered and spend little time talking about their concerns with other fathers or professionals. Dads tell us that they have not done much reading on the subject of ADHD, and there has never been a book written specifically for them about their relationship with their children. Those fathers who have sought out answers report having an enduring, unique, and special relationship with their child.

This book was written to answer your questions. While some background information on ADHD, child development, and parenting is presented, the main focus of the book is on your relationship with your child (or children) and how you can make it more rewarding and successful for both of you.

Chapter 1

WHAT ADHD IS
AND ISN'T

What is life? It is the flash of a firefly in the night. It is
the breath of a buffalo in the winter time; it is the
little shadow which runs across the grass and loses itself in the sunset.

Last words of Crowfoot

As illustrated in these last words of Crowfoot, sometimes it
is the ordinary things in life that are the most beautiful. Yet
because of our familiarity with them, we may not notice their
beauty. Children with ADHD are talented, bright, and gifted.
However, these wonderful traits can easily be overlooked.

ADHD can have an intense emotional impact on the child,
the parents, and the whole family. This impact, however, does
not have to be negative or damaging. With parental support,
ADHD can become the child's ally rather than adversary. It is
the responsibility of parents, and all of us who say we care, to protect the self-esteem, uniqueness, and beauty of every child. This
support is especially important for those living with ADHD.

Even though children with ADHD experience a wide range
of symptoms, they share similar behavioral and emotional reactions. Two fathers describe their sons' ADHD:

1

Even though Marty has ADHD, I see him as having an inability to attend more than having acute behavioral problems. I have heard of children with ADHD who are difficult to manage behaviorally. He doesn't fit that category. At age 11 he is a gifted athlete, a popular kid at school, and very charismatic. The area where he struggles most is maintaining his focus on what is required of him. He does pretty well in school, but often finds it boring and a major chore to do homework or read, even for pleasure. Because he is so capable, I ride him about finishing what he starts and taking more responsibility and care in completing things. Even though he has all this ability, it seems he doesn't feel as strong or good about himself as he should.

Sam is a talented kid, but he really tries my patience and the patience of the teachers at school. He tends not to listen. And when he feels overwhelmed, regardless of what it is, he becomes defensive and almost childlike. It is definitely not the behavior of an average 10-year-old. I find myself losing my temper and yelling or kind of putting him down. I honestly don't know how else to get through to him. After a blowup or screaming match, he'll come back and say he is sorry for being so bad. It pulls at my heart. He just seems like he has the weight of the world on his shoulders. Now that I think about it, maybe he does.

Fathers can help shape and direct the emotional destiny of all their children. Fathers of children with ADHD have a special calling: to stand with their children in their emotional or behavioral difficulties, to support them when they seem to be slipping emotionally or behaviorally, and to give their children hope, courage, and the opportunity to define themselves by their strengths rather than their weaknesses. To do this, it helps to try to look through the eyes of our children, to appreciate their experiences and the struggles they face.

Children with ADHD have to contend with their feelings

(and the world) in a way that is decidedly different from that of their peers. Their experiences in social and family situations often leave these children feeling vulnerable, different, and "bad." The feedback they receive from family members, teachers, peers, and even strangers tends to reinforce these feelings.

"Why can't you control yourself?"

"What's wrong with you?"

"You are always screwing things up!"

"What is your problem?"

"I am sick and tired of you!"

"Why can't you be like your brother or sister?"

"Why can't you act like Sara, Johnny, or the other children in the class?"

"You obviously don't want to participate, so sit in a chair in the corner until we are finished!"

"If you do that again, I guarantee you I'll smack you even harder."

"If you just try harder, maybe you'll be like the other kids in the class!"

"My son is afraid to be around little Peter because he can't play nice."

Children with ADHD hear comments like these daily. The feelings of inadequacy that these experiences create can shape their self-image. The damage this causes, however, can be diminished with parental support and intervention.

By nature, children are impulsive, egocentric, and curious. Their behaviors and thinking patterns are not governed by logic or adult etiquette. If you want to know the world of a child, watch a group of eight-year-old children playing together, trading baseball cards, arguing over kickball, and saying they will never be each other's friend again, yet ten minutes later, huddling together with the newest video game. Children interact and play according to a different social order from that of adults. They can be abrasive and insensitive one minute, incredibly compassionate another, and in the next, mean to their sibling Children with ADHD can be expected to act only like the children they are, not like miniature adults.

As another father said:

When we tell children that they are "bad" or "lazy" because of something they did, we are reinforcing in their mind that they are fundamentally flawed. Because their behavior does not line up with our adult expectations, our words and feelings begin to sculpt a caricature of who they are. A small piece of who they are is blown up into this ridiculous shape that does not represent reality. It is like the caricatures of people we see being painted on the boardwalk or in malls. At first glance the caricature is funny, only slightly resembling the reality of the individual. At closer inspection, caricatures, by their very nature, are insulting. They focus on and often distort irrelevant aspects of the person. Once completed, the caricature has virtually nothing in common with the individual being depicted.

This is what can happen when we focus too much on an aspect of our child's behavior. Our child's vision of himself can become like those mall caricatures—distorted and insulting.

Interventions such as medication, behavior management, or counseling sometimes create in parents false expectations for their child's behavior. This is illustrated by one father:

When Ricky was first medicated I couldn't believe the difference in his behavior. The transformation was dramatic. He went from this moody, hyper, distracted, and disagreeable kid to this young guy who was kind, focused, and helpful. After he was on medication for a while, my wife mentioned that I was being unreasonably hard on him. She thought I treated him better before he was medicated! As it turns out, I expected the medication to remove *all* the negative behavior. The minute he did something rude or wrong I was all over him.

Then one day I was talking with a buddy who said his son got mad earlier that morning and smacked his car with a pogo stick. I couldn't believe it. That sounded like something Ricky would do if he had a tantrum. And this was just a kid who didn't have ADHD or any of that. He got overwhelmed by his anger and lashed out. I know this sounds strange, but I learned a lot by this. I have to let Ricky be a kid, not some perfect robot who never does anything wrong, refuses to show his feelings, or won't take risks because he's afraid he'll be punished if it doesn't go right.

Like Ricky's dad, you can provide the emotional cushion necessary for your child to experience the daily success required to feel competent and secure. Providing this support may require a shift in your thinking about what to pay attention to and what to dismiss.

It may be helpful to know that when you are frustrated with your child's behavior, your child is also feeling the same level of frustration. At such a moment, your son may be momentarily frozen in time, like a deer caught in the headlights. His natural desire to please and conform is overshadowed by his emotional state, which he doesn't know how to fix. With each demand for him to "snap out of it" or indication that he is a disappointment, the pain sinks deeper and the "headlights" get brighter.

Strategies for supporting your child when he is having emotional or aggressive behaviors related to his ADHD are listed in Table 1. These strategies will provide productive and effective ways to deal with the intense emotions that you both feel.

Ignoring certain types of inappropriate behavior has proven the path of least resistance for many parents of children with

TABLE 1

Ways to Prevent Your Son's Aggressive or Overly Emotional Behavior

◆ Remain calm.

◆ Plan and discuss expectations before entering into situations. What are the expected behaviors? What are your family's behavioral rules? What can your child expect to encounter? How can your child deal with problems if they arise? What will be the rewards (if any) for appropriate behavior?

◆ Provide clear and consistent consequences (follow-through) for inappropriate or undesirable behavior.

◆ Slow the pace of an interaction and your intensity by presenting a relaxed and nonthreatening stance. Maintain eye contact; lower your vocal tone; gently touch the arm, if appropriate; acknowledge that your son is upset; invite him to work with you to develop an alternative to the situation.

◆ Remain flexible. This can help diffuse a troubled situation. Let your child participate in a discussion for finding an alternative, more appropriate behavior.

◆ Praise positive behaviors whenever possible (such as when your son hangs up his coat without being told to do it).

ADHD. However, you may fear that by ignoring a behavior, you will subtly reinforce it. It is important to remember that the majority of these children's negative behaviors emerge from an inability to conform, not from a willful desire to be disobedient. When we focus on positive behavior, we reinforce the behaviors that are under our sons' direct control. The more we acknowledge appropriate behavior, the more likely it will increase in strength and appearance. The same is true for negative behaviors. The more we concentrate on negative behaviors, the more our sons will learn to see themselves in that light and behave accordingly.

ADHD-related problems create stress and affect all members of the family. One father reminisced:

It wasn't until after my son started taking medication that I became aware of how stressful ADHD was on me and the rest of the family. Within a short period of time the endless tug-of-war and screaming bouts subsided significantly. I felt like we had all been paroled from a really bad place. Over time I learned to both see and treat my son very differently. He still has an occasional bad day, but that's all it is, a bad day—not a bad life! The combination of the medication and our working hard to treat each other with respect has given us a new lease on life. I learned to let go of a lot of the seemingly trivial stuff that used to tie me up in knots, resulting in my yelling or saying something hurtful. Before, when I would put on my serious face and tell him to do or not to do something, he would sometimes make this ridiculous face—the kind kids make when teasing each other. It would drive me absolutely crazy. Now, on the rare occasions he does this, instead of emotionally whirling around the room, I simply and calmly let him know that is not appropriate, and I drop it. That is a completely different reaction than a year ago. It is amazing that as I have changed, so has my son—it has made all the difference in the world.

When you pay attention to positive behaviors, and either ignore or calmly deal with the negative behaviors, you create a major shift in the way your child will see himself and the world. Training yourself to ignore impulsive or inappropriate behavior requires an understanding of what your son can—and can't—control. If you reinforce the positive movements toward success, that is how your child will begin to define himself—as a success!

When you become more accepting of your child's behavior, a paradox occurs: the problematic behavior diminishes in frequency, intensity, and duration. We are not suggesting you accept the inappropriate behavior, but rather that you accept your son for who he is and for what he can and cannot do. This does not mean ADHD is or can be used as an excuse for acting out or engaging in disrespectful behaviors. As will be discussed in later chapters, we can hold our children accountable for their behavior while still maintaining a position of love and support.

Personal control over ADHD symptoms generally comes with physical and emotional maturity, well-constructed intervention and treatment strategies, and a consistent and healthy parent-child relationship. You can and must set clear limits on what will and will not be tolerated. However, the way these limits are enforced will often determine the stress level of your son, yourself, and your family.

JUST WHAT IS ADHD?

What is ADHD? Why does your son act the way he does? If your son had a broken arm or diabetes, you would be able to take him to a doctor, and an X-ray or a blood test would show you what problem was causing the trouble. But this is not the case with ADHD. While considerable research has been done on ADHD over the past several decades, as yet no single bio-

**Your son may feel frozen in time,
like a deer caught in the headlights. (page 5)**

logical cause has been found to explain all of the symptoms we
commonly see. However, new technology, such as the MRI and
PET scans, has shown that individuals with ADHD exhibit distinct neurological and biochemical brain functioning.

With ADHD, areas of the brain that are responsible for in-
hibiting behaviors, incorporating rules, planning ahead, or fig-
uring out solutions do not work the way they should. Lack of
inhibition often results in the complex set of behaviors seen in
ADHD. Because these may change day by day, or even minute
to minute, as a result of the brain's unique biochemistry, your
child's behaviors and emotional responses may be unpredictable to you and to himself. This inconsistency in performance
is naturally confusing and disappointing to both you and your
child. Because you have seen him behave appropriately in some
situations, you expect your child to be capable of the same be-

havior at all times. Unfortunately, this is not the case. The one thing that we can conclude with certainty is that the most predictable thing about ADHD is its unpredictability.

When your child's behavior seems out of control, it is important to remember what is causing it. He can no more control his brain functioning or behavioral response than he can regulate his blood sugar level or heal his broken arm simply by willing it.

There are many causes of ADHD, but the most common is probably genetic. Studies of identical and fraternal twins have found a significantly higher incidence of ADHD in identical twins. In another study, more cases of ADHD were found in relatives of children with ADHD than in the relatives of children who did not have ADHD. This is why we see many fathers and sons who both have ADHD. Since ADHD seems to have some biological basis, several children in a family may experience some degree of ADHD.

HOW DO I KNOW IF MY CHILD HAS ADHD?

Despite the fact that we now know a considerable amount about ADHD and the involvement of certain areas of the brain, the diagnosis continues to be based on personal history and the presence of certain behavioral and emotional characteristics. A physician or mental health professional makes the diagnosis after interviews with the parents, the child, and school personnel. Extensive neuropsychological testing may also be performed to establish the diagnosis and determine if there are also learning disabilities. The professional must rule out other causes for the symptoms such as depression, a conduct disorder, or oppositional-defiant disorder. There are, as yet, no blood tests to confirm the diagnosis of ADHD. While brain scans are used in research, they are not currently available for diagnostic purposes.

In order to standardize the diagnosis of behavior disorders, the American Psychiatric Association has published a manual with criteria for each diagnosis. This is called *The Diagnostic and Statistical Manual of Mental Disorders*, 4th edition (DSM-IV). This latest version was published in 1994. According to the DSM-IV, the diagnosis of ADHD requires a persistent (at least six months) pattern of symptoms of inattention and/or hyperactivity and impulsivity. These symptoms must have been present before the age of seven years and in at least two settings, such as school and home. Table 2 lists symptoms that might be seen in your son if he has ADHD.

TABLE 2

Symptoms of ADHD in Children

◆ Has difficulty paying attention.

◆ Makes "careless" mistakes.

◆ Doesn't seem to listen.

◆ Doesn't follow instructions well.

◆ Avoids tasks that require a sustained mental effort such as schoolwork or homework.

◆ Forgets to do chores.

◆ Has difficulty organizing tasks or activities.

◆ Frequently loses toys, books, clothing, tools, etc.

◆ Is forgetful in daily activities.

◆ Impulsively blurts out answers or interrupts.

◆ Has difficulty waiting his turn in conversations or games.

◆ Fidgets or squirms in his seat.

In effect, he has no brakes and can't stop an activity or reflect on a behavior before acting. Your son frequently doesn't learn from his mistakes.

WHAT ADHD IS NOT

As we now know, ADHD is a neurologically based condition. It is <u>not</u> caused by poor parenting or too little discipline. ADHD affects your son's ability to control impulses, focus on pertinent information in a consistent fashion, and regulate his activity level. ADHD is <u>not</u> a conduct disorder, oppositional-defiant disorder, or other type of severe behavior problem.

However, if left untreated into adolescence or young adulthood, ADHD can lead to severe behavioral problems. If children remain in an emotionally and psychologically unsupportive environment, the years of negative messages, underachievement, and emotional pain can easily cause them to become defiant, antisocial, and bitter. But how do you prevent ADHD from becoming a larger problem? Table 3 offers some suggestions for addressing this issue.

It cannot be stated strongly enough that, given the right type of help and emotional support, your son can do as well or better than his peers who do not have ADHD!

The behavior of children with ADHD can sometimes mimic that of children who have conduct disorder (CD) or oppositional-defiant disorder (ODD). One father noted:

When Paul is off his medication and his emotions are swirling all around, if I say something that irritates him, which isn't hard to do, he'll immediately say something like "Shut up" or "Get out of my face." It took me a while to accept the fact that that is his impulsive side showing. At that moment he really can't control what he is saying. When he is

TABLE 3

How to Prevent ADHD from Becoming a Larger Problem

◆ Avoid being insensitive, dismissive, or abusive toward your child.

◆ Avoid frequent and hurtful negative comments toward your child, such as, "You know, you are such a screwup. No wonder no one wants to be around you."

◆ Avoid physically hitting or verbally condemning your child.

◆ Provide consistent supervision of your child's activities. An uncaring and unsupportive attitude can lead to your child's antisocial behavior.

◆ Avoid modeling inappropriate or abusive problem-solving or conflict resolution strategies, such as, excessive substance use and abuse, chronic yelling, emotional volatility, emotional withdrawal, or parental absence.

on medication, that type of response is very rare. I also respond to it very differently now, so he doesn't hang onto the negative feeling. I can tell he wants to say or do something different, but this surge happens and he blurts out this stuff. Since my attitude has changed, the more negative impulsive responses happen far less frequently.

Paul's behavior could easily be confused with ODD, but since it is not willful in nature, it is not ODD. Of course, all children behave this way at one time or another. They lose their temper, act spiteful, and blame others, but children with ODD do so more often than is appropriate for their age. Children with ADHD also tend to behave this way more frequently than do those who do not have ADHD or ODD. If left unchecked, negative tendencies in children with ADHD can make the leap from impulsive behavior to an ingrained character trait.

Conduct disorder may be seen in children who are subjected to ongoing emotional, physical, or sexual abuse, or who consistently witness parents or guardians subjected to physical and emotional abuse, such as being hit by a spouse, screaming as the main means of verbal expression, or other verbal abuse. These then become the child's primary models for solving problems. Conduct disorder can also be seen in children who have an alcoholic parent. The combination of ongoing abuse in the family and inadequate parental supervision can lead to serious behavioral disturbances.

Children with ADHD may also develop serious behavior problems if they do not receive adequate support and attention to their needs. The difference between children who have ODD, CD, and ADHD is that children with ADHD *do not willfully* disobey or try to create conflict in their lives and the lives of those around them. When children with ADHD act inappropriately or irresponsibly, it is usually because of incompetence (they cannot at that moment do otherwise), not deliberate disobedience. They can, however, become deliberately disobedient over time if experience teaches them that is how their families and the world view them.

WHAT CAN YOU DO?

As a father, you have a very important role. As your son develops cognitively, emotionally, and behaviorally, your support, acceptance, and belief will be the lantern by which he will light his path. With your intervention and support, his own personal successes, and time, his ADHD will become more manageable. According to one father:

I have seen Quint use many of the techniques or strategies that my wife and I have used with him over the years. If he is getting too aggressive or angry, he pulls himself temporarily out of the situation to cool down, focus, and figure out what exactly is going on—and how he is contributing to the problem. We are starting to see the results of years of working with him, modeling for him, and standing by him. When he was first diagnosed at age four, he was aggressive, agitated, and difficult to control. Now at age eight, he still has his down moments, but it is nothing compared to what it was. I see Quint as a happy and self-confident young boy. Because he was so disruptive at an early age, it would have been easy to be angry and disapproving of him a lot. But with guidance, talking with other parents, and professional help, Quint is, and is going to be, fine. Each day he learns to cope with ADHD more effectively.

This is a wonderful example of how even the most difficult ADHD temperament can respond positively to sound parental structure and ongoing support. It is when we get caught up in our sons' emotional and behavioral dramas that we limit our ability to keep the path well lit by creating a safe and understanding environment. But how can a father set limits for his son that will create this positive environment? Table 4 presents some suggestions.

TABLE 4

How to Set Limits for Your Son and Create a Positive Environment in Your Family

◆ Be clear about and discuss often family values, such as that littering is unacceptable, smoking harms a person's health, etc.

◆ Discuss each person's obligation to one another and the family. Make clear what is expected of each person, what it takes to make your family run well, etc.

◆ Be clear about and discuss what is *not* acceptable in the family, such as being mean to a sibling, lying, cheating, etc.

◆ Be clear about what consequences will be associated with specific behaviors, also what rewards will accompany specific behaviors.

◆ Follow-through and consistency are fundamental in minimizing problems. If you say it—mean it. And if you mean it—do it. Remember to think about what response will most likely motivate your son to behave the way you want. Angry or irrational responses by you will only serve to heighten his anxiety and confusion.

Chapter 2

HOW ADHD AFFECTS PARENTING

Life is difficult.

M. Scott Peck
The Road Less Traveled

Life consists of an interplay of the bitter and the sweet. Along with the wonderful moments, accomplishments, and personal achievements come difficult challenges, which can sometimes feel heavy and burdensome. However, we should not ignore or shrink from life's uncomfortable moments, for it is precisely the difficult experiences that teach us about who and what we are.

Like life, parenting is difficult! All parents worry about their children. Will they grow up to be good citizens? Will they make the same mistakes I made? Will they be accepted by teachers and peers? Will they achieve their potential? Will they be able to surmount life's daily tests, chores, and problems? As one father noted:

One of the major things I see blocking the relationship I have with my son is my response to him when he is doing something inappropriate or wrong. Or at least what I think is inappropriate or wrong! When I see him loafing at practice or spending 30 minutes to memorize five spelling words, I move into this very critical or unsupportive space. I know he can do better. So I tend to ridicule him in hope that the negative feelings will motivate him to act differently. I have noticed that, in fact, the opposite happens. He feels beaten down and betrayed to a degree. It seems during the times when he could use my encouragement or support, he gets stepped on. It's strange really—the one thing I don't want to see happen, him feel bad about himself, becomes reinforced when I treat him this way. I have also noticed that when I let go of my fears about what he "will become" and support him where he is at, his attitude makes a noticeable shift—to something more positive.

As you know, parenting is not an exact science. What seems to be an effective and positive parenting strategy one day may have a negative effect the next day. For instance, your son is studying his spelling words for a quiz on Friday morning. You say, "Ten more minutes, take a practice test, and then you can go play." He agrees, focuses hard for ten minutes, takes his test, and is off to play. The next day, however, you say the same thing, in the same tone, and he becomes agitated, whiny, and argumentative. "I don't want to study ten more minutes, I want to go play now. I promise I'll do it later. Why do you always make me do this? I hate this!" What changed? Certainly not your tone of voice or your expectations. Your son's mood and frame of emotional reference changed, which compromised the type of interaction you wanted to have with your son. The expectations you presented to him seemed both reasonable and familiar. But he, it seemed, "decided" to become obstinate and unyielding.

In fact, a child who has ADHD does not "decide" on his emotion, but rather experiences a "wave of emotion carrying him away from the shores of reason." This wave can have a crushing effect on your immediate interaction. You may get mad and yell, or make a threat like "You cannot go out for the rest of the day," only to let him go out an hour later after your anger has settled. Avoiding these types of interaction is possible if certain strategies are followed. Table 5 offers some suggestions to consider when confronted with an intense emotional situation.

One father compared parenting his son who has ADHD with riding a roller coaster:

Lenny is such a charismatic, intense, and interesting boy. When we are getting along, it's like being on top of a roller coaster, things couldn't be better. However, there is a part of me that tends to anticipate the quick fall or plummet to the bottom. The rush, the fear, the tension, the feeling of being off balance . . . I noticed that as I learn to anticipate it, I become anxious, short-tempered, and more demanding. It stands to reason that as I start becoming more anxious, so will he. I am not saying I cause the emotional plummet or tension, but I do think I contribute to it and at times fan the flame. I also notice that when I meet those emotional plummets with reason, calm, and support, they are less intense and last for a very short time. I see big gains in extending my arm for support rather than the back of my hand for conformity.

Parenting calls us to a level of responsibility unparalleled in any other area of our life. Our children are more than an extension of us, they represent all the possibilities and potential the world has to offer. They have the opportunity to exceed our expectations and to excel in unimaginable directions. We place enormous responsibility on our children to succeed, make good choices, establish sound values, and be good citizens. We often

TABLE 5

Promoting Better Interactions with Your Son

◆ Intense emotions are often difficult for a child with ADHD to describe or even contain. His emotions spill out in inappropriate ways, or the intensity of the emotion is out of proportion to the situation. You can help your son regain balance if you acknowledge his feelings. For example, you can say, "It seems like it was really hard for you to hear 'no' just now," and then ignore the intensity or meet his intensity with a calm voice and subdued attitude.

◆ Permit your son to come and talk with you when he is ready rather than when you want him to. After children with ADHD explode or act defiant, they realize quickly what they have done and often want to talk about it. Even if you are still angry at your son's behavior, letting him come to you when he is ready signals you are open to his desire to act more appropriately.

◆ If your son's behavior makes you angry, you can acknowledge that his behavior is bothering you, that it is inappropriate, and that if it continues, he will have to be in time-out. This keeps you from exploding and sets clear limits for your son.

◆ Give your son as much warning as possible before a sanction. This also signals you that you are reaching your limit and that you are taking steps to avoid exploding.

expect them to capitalize on opportunities we failed to or were unable to, and to construct a magnificent staircase carrying them to their and, by extension, our individual success. We want them to heal our historical wounds. In reality, however, our children must battle the same battles we fought, feel the same disappointments we felt, and learn the way we did to make sense out of an unpredictable world.

However, your child does not have to face the world entirely alone; he has you as a guiding force. While our children *may* offer us an opportunity to heal, what they definitely offer us is the chance to live honestly, demonstrate integrity, model forgiveness, show compassion, and basically live what it means to be human. We can give our children the things, emotional and physical, we did not get. As many parents have learned over the ages, it is much easier to provide physical comforts than the emotional comfort we may not have received ourselves. Fathers, especially, must push against both gender and social stereotypes in order to provide their children, and especially their sons with ADHD, with the level of emotional sustenance they need.

THE SHIP'S CAPTAIN

No one likes to feel out of control, especially a child who is not yet equipped with the cognitive and emotional resolve to soothe himself and put things in perspective. Children turn to their parents to learn their level of worthiness. It may be helpful to consider your parenting role as similar to that of a ship's captain. The captain does not assert his will against the forces of nature, but rather works with and respects the forces he encounters. By the way he sets his sails, he uses the power of the winds to guide the vessel. In parenting sons, there are times when the forces of their nature are so powerful that we must bend our will and desires to preserve the integrity and safety of the ship. If the captain disregards the warning signs that nature imparts, or asserts his will against that of nature, there is usually some type of damage.

As the forces of nature determine a ship captain's decisions, so do our sons provide us with behavioral or attitudinal signals indicating the most effective way to set our sails. If a father demands that his son act in a desired way or control himself in a particular setting, without checking out his son's emotional climate, the father may be disregarding the telltale signs that would help avoid conflict and regret. Accommodating the nature of our children does not mean giving in to their every whim or desire. It does not mean we cannot expect certain behaviors. It does mean that we can meet their feelings of frustration and being overwhelmed with calm and supportive responses. This approach serves to right a listing ship and give the child encouragement, security, and feelings of belonging. It is also important to acknowledge that being the voice of reason and a calming influence on your child can be enormously difficult when he has pushed your emotional buttons to the limit.

The following story provides us with insight into what happens in a father and son relationship when the father no longer demands that "his will be done," but rather respects and is guided by the needs of his son who has ADHD.

TONY'S STORY

Growing up in a very ethnic Italian household, I learned when my father said to do something, it better be done or we would get one of his "lessons on responsibility." This usually entailed being hit or spanked several times. My father had very little tolerance for disobedience or asserting your own will. He would hold court every night at dinner telling wild stories and howling about life's injustices. The energy of everyone in the family had to match his. I mean, if he asked you to tell a story or do something, you needed to respond immediately. And you couldn't finish until he was satisfied. He was always someone that everyone feared and revered. He died when I was eleven, so the impression I have always had of him is this larger-than-life figure. Since my mother never remarried, I never had any other intense exposure to how other fathers deal with their families and sons. I don't want to give you the impression that my father was a mean man; he was just very clear about how he wanted things to operate in the family.

This reflection on my father is important and related to how I parent and feel about my two sons, Adrian and Marc. I remember fearing my father, so rarely did I ever disrespect him or be disobedient to him. My mom, on the other hand, was a different story. I would frequently use her as my emotional whipping post. She often protected me from Dad by not telling him about my back talking or problems in school. Although I am a bright guy, I found school to be a heavy burden. It always seemed I was having a problem in one area or another. Even in sports I had a hard time following the rules. I suppose my mom would say I was a handful.

I remember on many occasions in college thinking about what type of dad I would be, how I would be so different from my father, and the limitless things I would do with my children. I remember specific instances when I literally saw myself with these little kids who loved me and always wanted to be with me because I listened to them, never yelled, and appreciated who and what they were. I believed that because I wanted children and was committed to being a good and available dad, my kids would feel great about life, themselves, and the family.

I remember being with my wife in the hospital as we prepared to have our first child. We knew it was a boy from the ultrasound tests, so I had several months to anticipate the day of his birth. When Adrian was born, it was magical. I felt, really felt, now I will be able to have the kind of relationship with my son that I did not have with my dad. I am not going to make the same mistakes. I thought, I am not my father—I am my son's dad. That was an incredibly powerful feeling. Maybe it is because I lost my dad when I was young, or I always wanted more

Parenting a son with ADHD is like riding a roller coaster. (page 19)

from him when he was alive, that I believed the arrival of Adrian was the answer to a lot of the questions I had about myself since I was young.

The first year of being a parent was exactly as I envisioned it would be: Adrian was a great baby who we took everywhere with us. We traveled, went a lot of places. He was a great little traveler and companion. He loved people and rarely fussed when a stranger picked him up. As he grew and matured, at around a year and a half or two, it was evident that Adrian didn't listen well to what my wife and I would say. If he was expected to do something he didn't want to do or like to do, he would have tantrums—which were embarrassing when we were in public. It seemed his favorite word was "no." He was cute and fun, but there was this side to him that was not only concerning us but definitely agitating us. If my father said do something, you did it. It was not open for discussion. Adrian seemed increasingly to have a hard time having limits set on him. I am not talking unreasonable limits. I mean, "Hey, Adrian, it's time for a bath before bed," and at three-years-old he would lose it. It began to be a real struggle to do anything normal with him.

When we put him in daycare at age three, the daycare provider said he had a lot of energy and seemed to move from one thing to another without finishing anything. I thought he was just three and a boy, so that was normal. When we put him in preschool at four, however, the teachers said that he did not follow the rules the way the other children did. He rarely finished a task or sat long enough to listen to a book. After two preschools, we decided to seek professional help. Through a series of meetings and testings, it was determined that Adrian had ADHD. I wasn't sure what it was, but it was a medical diagnosis, which I lamented couldn't be very promising. Also at this time Adrian had a brother, Marc, who had just turned one.

I remember sitting in the doctor's office, staring out the window, wondering what I had done wrong. The images of the past several months came into my mind when I had been yelling at and punishing Adrian, just as my father did to me. I remember feeling very empty and alone. Even though the doctor talked about the positive sides of ADHD, and that it is something that could be controlled through medication and behavior programs, I heard and accepted very little of it.

Time went by and the relationship I had with Adrian seemed pretty strained. My wife and I would frequently have arguments about how to handle Adrian. I felt that he was being disobedient, while my wife felt he couldn't help it. I thought maybe my father was right. Maybe I had to be rigid and aloof to get through to this kid. It seemed no matter what I did, it was never good enough for Adrian. He seemed to have a continual problem with what I did or didn't do. This was not the way I thought things would be. In many ways I was becoming my father to my son.

When Adrian was five we started going to CH.A.D.D. meetings, which are support groups for parents who have kids with ADHD. I can honestly say attending CH.A.D.D. started opening my eyes to how difficult ADHD is on Adrian, and how essential it was that my wife and I act as his ballast and support him.

CHALLENGES AND OPPORTUNITIES

Children with ADHD present us daily with challenges, but also with opportunities for personal growth. As one father stated:

I was a marine in Vietnam, struggled through starting and succeeding at opening my own business, but very little has touched my heart and my fury like the behaviors associated with ADHD.

◆ ◆ ◆

ADHD requires that we operate at a fairly consistent and rational level. This can be incredibly difficult with a disorder that plays on the emotions of both the child and the family.

We can find comfort in knowing that the extra time we spend with our sons, and the extra effort we expend to understand them, will have a lasting positive effect on their overall development. Children with ADHD need more from their parents to successfully paddle through the turbulent waters of childhood. They need more time to complete tasks, more reminders, more attention, more understanding, more of just about everything. This can exhaust even the most attentive and well-intentioned parent.

This is especially true when there are siblings or both parents have stressful and demanding jobs. We have a finite amount of energy and patience to accommodate the needs of our children. Amidst all these demands, these children need to know on a regular basis that they are okay. Children with ADHD have developed a heightened sense of awareness of when people's words match their behaviors. They may feel the parent is not interested in them, when in fact the parent is tired from a long day or is preoccupied with work-related business.

Because ADHD is often so emotionally intense and the level of internal distraction is so high, these children have a tendency to disconnect emotionally with the immediate situation. One father describes this phenomena:

Early this morning my son got angry at my wife. He stormed up the stairs, and, as I was standing in the middle of the room in my boxers, he leans in the doorway on the way to his room and says, "I hate you Dad," and then disappears to his room. I had nothing to do with the situation. This strange kind of event is not unusual in our house. I am not sure what to do, so I say, "Boy, it seems like your really upset right now." I don't get angry, I just reflect what I see happening.

◆ ◆ ◆

Chapter 3

HOW ADHD AFFECTS FATHERS

Life can only be understood backwards, but it must
be lived forwards.

Soren Kierkegaard

ADHD has a way of cutting through rational thought processes, feeding directly into paternal emotions and anger. All
parents, as all people, can reach a "saturation point" where they
run out of patience. It is difficult to remain rational in the face
of certain behaviors associated with ADHD. Even parents who
are relatively well-informed on the most effective ways to manage ADHD, like the fathers we spoke to, acknowledge moments
of intolerance and impatience that result in an emotional erup-
tion of their own. While it is important to know the effects of
ADHD on our children in order to help them through the difficulties it causes, it is just as important to understand the effects
of your son's ADHD on you, the father.

Once a father realizes he has had or is going to have a little
boy, thoughts start racing through his mind: "Will he be healthy?
Will he be smart? Will he grow to love the things that are important to me? Am I going to be a good dad? What will it be like

having a son?" These questions, and many more, are natural in preparing to be a parent. Unless the child is born with a visible and undeniable disability, a father often thinks about his son's development in terms of his own childhood, and what it means to be a boy in today's society. A father then begins to develop expectations about how his son will function in the family and the world. The temperament of the child and his receptivity to the father will shape these expectations. One father remembers the first 18 months of his son's life as being terrific:

Jon was the best baby you could ask for. He wasn't overly fussy, and we could comfortably take him just about anywhere. I enjoyed being around him and rarely had to raise my voice or get upset with him. After 18 months, something changed. He was always very active, but he became defiant, for lack of a better term. He wouldn't listen, he was very clingy, he couldn't sit and entertain himself without my wife or I being there, he was into everything he wasn't supposed to be, he had very little control over his activity level, and he had unbelievable tantrums. It felt like he had changed overnight. I noticed becoming more stressed around him, and our time together wasn't very much fun. It seemed everything was a hassle. I really expected this close relationship to keep developing as he grew older. What happened was that it became increasingly difficult. I can also say that along with being angry, I felt a real sense of loss and dismay that I wasn't going to have the type of relationship I expected.

Every father wants his son to be affectionate, but not clingy; even tempered, not emotionally volatile and inconsistent; outgoing, but not overly demanding; curious, but not moving from one thing to another without completing anything; daring, but not without internal or external control; assertive, but not inappropriately aggressive toward others. Most children with ADHD cannot live up to these expectations or even approximate them without intervention and treatment. Even with treatment, the behaviors related to ADHD are only managed—they do not disappear as a headache does after one takes an aspirin.

The temperament of the child is of paramount importance. It will often determine the quality of response from the father. Children with difficult temperaments, like children with ADHD, may have fathers who are critical and angry, or distant and removed. Even when children receive outside help to alleviate some of their difficulties, they still will have characteristics that at times are distancing.

When a father makes a conscious effort to adjust his expectations for his son, a more positive and equally reinforcing relationship begins to develop. As one father said:

Once I accepted that Mitch is who he is, and is not going to be immediately what I expected him to be, my attitude toward him became more forgiving. I think he sees I really care, and I am not pushing him the way I used to. Pushing him to achieve, or to pay attention, or to like the things I like was the wrong approach with him. Now that I have backed off, things are less strained. I also enjoy him much more and we have better times together.

Another father described reevaluating his expectations of his son:

I can't expect Philip to respect me if I don't respect him or support him. He knows just by my looks when I disapprove of him or am angry. I don't mean disapprove of him, but disapprove of his behaviors. Actually, I used to disapprove of *him,* and he knew it. If I expect him to "honor thy father," I must honor him. I am the point man here, and where I go, he will follow. The medication and behavior techniques have helped me make my expectations more realistic.

◆ ◆ ◆

We must not underestimate the change that can occur in a son when his father retools his expectations to fall in line with his son's temperament and specific needs. If we try to rush our sons' development, or become impatient with their unique styles of growing and learning, we run the risk of dampening or even extinguishing a vital part of them and, along the way, sabotaging the relationship. We must allow things to unfold according to their own development and time. We can encourage that development, but it can be dangerous if we push it too fast and too far:

> I remember one morning when I discovered a cocoon in the bark of a tree, just as the butterfly was making a hole in the case and preparing to come out. I waited a while, but it was too long appearing and I was impatient. I bent over it and breathed on it to warm it. I warmed it as fast as I could and the miracle began to happen before my eyes, faster than life. The case opened, the butterfly started slowly crawling out and I shall never forget my horror when I saw how its wings were folded back and crumpled; the wretched butterfly tried with its whole trembling body to unfold them. Bending over it, I tried to help with my breath. In vain. It needed to be hatched out patiently and the unfolding of the wings should be a gradual process in the sun. Now it was too late. My breath had forced the butterfly to appear, all crumpled, before its time. It struggled desperately, and, a few seconds later, died in the palm of my hand.
>
> That little body is, I do believe, the greatest weight I have on my conscience . . . We should not hurry, we should not be impatient, but we should confidently obey the external rhythm.
>
> Nikos Kazantzakis, *Zorba the Greek*

We must likewise permit our sons to unfold according to their abilities and interests. Children with ADHD tend to be slower in "emerging from the cocoon" than their peers. If we continue to breathe down their backs, it is hard for their potential and innate talent to unfold. Often the perspective of the parent makes the difference between a child who feels "crumpled" and one whose "wings are ready for flight." Understanding the developmental aspects of your son's behavior is important for making judgments about what he can and cannot be asked to do. Table 6 expands on this concept.

PASSING THE BATON

Many of the fathers we talked to mentioned feeling some guilt or shame about how they have dealt with their sons' ADHD. Some felt responsible for saddling their child with ADHD:

I feel like I have condemned my son to a life of emotional and social struggle. I had ADHD when I was a child, or at least I think I did, and now my son has to contend with the same issues and feel the same kind of feelings. I don't want him to feel the internal angst I felt, but I really don't know what to do.

Even though I somehow feel responsible for my son's problems, I know I can give him the support I didn't receive when I was dealing with the same issues at his age. It's hard, though, because his behavior can really stir up a lot of anger in me.

Other fathers felt they were exceedingly (and often unnecessarily) hard on their sons during times when their impulsive behavior could not have been controlled:

TABLE 6

Understanding the Developmental Aspects of Your Son's Behavior

◆ ADHD generally results in a child being more emotionally immature than his peers. This means that his responses may be less sophisticated and more like a younger child.

◆ These immature or inappropriate responses have a neurological basis. Your son is not "not acting his age" deliberately or willfully.

◆ It will take your son longer than his peers to organize his thoughts, follow through on a task, and achieve at an age-appropriate level.

◆ Your son will not notice or respond immediately to logical cause-and-effect relationships, for example, that not picking up after himself will result in a loss of privilege or a time-out. Peers will make the connection sooner than your son. So be patient!

◆ Because of his internal confusion and neurological delays, your son will have much more difficulty following through on school assignments, paying attention to pertinent information, and achieving at the intellectual level indicated by testing.

◆ Your son knows long before you respond to his behavior that he has done something wrong. Your response serves either to gently instruct and encourage change, or to whittle away at his self-esteem.

◆ ◆ ◆

I wish, I mean really, really wish, I knew then what I know now. I know this sounds like some type of country-and-western song, but early on, even after he was diagnosed with ADHD, I still believed he was intentionally being irresponsible or disobedient. Because of this, I would grab him, scream at him, ridicule his choices and behavior, and basically just not support him. All the while, I was chiseling away the already-limited amount of self-esteem he had. I guess I wanted to believe he was choosing to be defiant, rather than incapable of doing what he knew was right. Reading about ADHD, I learned that there was nothing more he wanted than to be accepted and acceptable. The car was ready to go; there was just no gas in the engine.

◆ ◆ ◆

Not all fathers have first-hand experience or knowledge of ADHD prior to their sons' diagnoses. While ADHD is believed to be most often inherited (meaning that either a parent or a relative had similar problems while growing up), it is not exclusively biological in origin. And sometimes it is the mother who has ADHD:

I grew up as a fairly well-adjusted kid who played sports, did well in school, had a lot of friends, and rarely got in trouble other than what kids normally do. My father was a very calming influence in the house. He was a musician who spent a lot of time playing music with us and teaching us. I really can't think of any relatives offhand who had difficulties like my son, Ed. My wife, on the other hand, is pretty excitable, and she recalls having a tough time in school paying attention and following the rules. Emotionally, my wife has a rougher time dealing with Eddy because they both get worked up, and she loses control as much as he does.

Parents face tough choices on a daily basis. As parents of children with ADHD, we must also deal with our own strong emotions, reactions, and beliefs about our ADHD children from moment to moment. Counterpart to the guilt and anger that accompany parenting a child with ADHD are the many and varied opportunities for positive and healthy interventions and interactions.

I feel lucky to be able to deal with issues now that I didn't deal with when I was younger. I had no context to deal with them. Back then, hyperactive kids were labeled as lazy, stupid, or self-centered. I think people, including my parents, thought my behavior was related to bad parenting. They didn't understand how to deal with it. I am just beginning to, myself.

♦ ♦ ♦

While ADHD is not caused by poor or ineffective parenting, its symptoms can be amplified and made worse if parents try strong-arming their children into behaving, conforming, or "doing what they are supposed to." If children with ADHD have low self-esteem, it is difficult for them to muster the courage or resolve to do what is expected. They may find themselves caught in a cycle of "living down" to the expectations of others by continuing their inappropriate or troubling behavior. Feeling that they can do nothing right, they begin living out the belief that they are flawed.

Parents are in the most obvious position to keep their children from falling down the "slippery slope" of failure and self-recrimination. For a child to "buy in" to wanting to work on the problems related to ADHD requires a belief that his father will react supportively when problems emerge. A father with ADHD described the opportunity he sees in having a son who also has ADHD:

♦ ♦ ♦

When I was growing up, they didn't know what was wrong with me, other than that I could be really disagreeable and didn't follow rules very much. I was a nice kid and all, but I never really followed the program—whatever program it may have been. My dad frequently called me a "pain in the ass" and a "worthless kid." To some degree, I grew up believing what he said. I rarely internally celebrated any victory or positive thing I did. I remember thinking, "If I can do it, it must not be too great." My dad would say, when I did something good, "It's about time you did something besides get in trouble."

On the other hand, when I first became a father, I was determined to have a different relationship with my son than my father had with me. Petey has always been fidgety, distracted, and on-the-go. He can also be very charming and compassionate. It would have been easy to lock in to the negative behaviors and stuff, like my dad did, but I have chosen to give him a solid structure, make the rules of the house known, ignore stuff that pisses me off unless his safety or someone else's safety is a stake, and meet him where he is at. In order to do this, it required looking at my own childhood, my own temper, and what I really want for my son.

I can honestly say we now have a better relationship than I thought was possible a couple of years ago. I still worry about him, and it makes me sad when he makes impulsive or poor decisions, but we can talk about it and plan how things can be different next time. There are also times when I just sit next to him with my arms around him and say nothing. A lot of it depends on what he needs at the moment.

As a kid, after I got in trouble or disappointed my dad, he always used to say, "What goes around comes around." With Petey, I use this same phrase, but in a whole different way. I tell him it means that he will have another chance to do it differently in the future. I tell him it will come around again, and when it does, you can choose to act differently. I like my interpretation a lot better.

❖ ❖ ❖

PERSEVERANCE PAYS OFF

The type and degree of problems you must face on a daily basis as a father with a son with ADHD are often beyond the comprehension of most parents. There is an ongoing tension between wanting to love your son and wanting to give him away. One dad wondered:

Sometimes I feel like maybe he would be better off somewhere else. He seems unhappy a lot—not depressed, just really unhappy, like things don't go his way. I try my best to be there and do things with him, but it seems I never do it the right way or do it enough. I am not sure how to make him happy or more appreciative of the things he does have.

It may be helpful to know that the frustration you feel in meeting the needs of your son who has ADHD mirrors the tension and frustration your son feels in both expressing and meeting his own needs. These children have difficulty controlling and moderating the changes in their emotions and the environment. They frequently feel overwhelmed by their rapidly shifting needs and the often negative feedback they receive from those around them. In the words of one father:

Parenting Paul is similar to watching the funny-car races on ESPN. You see the cars on the starting line quivering and rumbling because of the powerful engines that make up the bulk of the car. You feel this tension from the car, as if it is screaming for the opportunity to fly down the track. Once they get the green light, they set off wildly with everything they have. Some spin out of control, some fly right past the checkered flag into oblivion, and others are able to somehow hold it together and successfully cross the finish line. With Paul, it used to be we would never know if he were going to crash and burn. Now, it's rare for him to blow past the checkered flag, or to have a blowout. His energy is much more controlled and directed. Much of it is due to the way I handle him and spend time with him.

It is important to note that even slight shifts in your interaction with your son can produce promising results for both of you. Frequently, we will invite parents who are emotionally running on fumes to learn more about how they interact with their children before we recommend any specific behavior management strategy. We ask the parents to do the following for one week:

Keep an "interaction journal" close by during the times you are with your son and write down in the journal four specific things:

1. The situation you and your child are involved in. (For example, going for ice cream after a baseball game.)

2. That part of the event that makes you feel angry or frustrated. (For example, when your son says, "I want the pint of ice cream, not a large cup! You are so unfair, you said I could get what I wanted.")

3. Your response. (For example, "Why are you such a brat, do you think everyone gets ice cream? You don't appreciate anything. Now you get nothing!")

4. Your son's reaction to your response. (For example, a screaming match that ensues or his becoming verbally out of control.)

It is important that you write exactly what you remember feeling and how you responded to the situation. This will help you become an expert in understanding how you currently deal with your son and what his reactions are to those interactions.

Finally, describe your actions when your son does something appropriate and positive. How does he respond to that feedback?

The next time we meet, we discuss the situations, feelings, and responses that occurred. Parents quickly begin to notice the patterns in their interaction that are problematic. They also recognize the way in which they either do or do not reinforce their son when he is acting appropriately and demonstrating self-control. This exercise can begin to reduce parents' emotional frustration. One father described using this exercise:

This very simple exercise opened my eyes to a number of things. Most importantly, I realized how unclear I frequently was with my son. I assumed he understood my expectations for a particular activity or what we were going to do. I noticed I rarely discussed what we were going to be doing, his expectations, my expectations, etc. It dawned on me halfway through this exercise that being aware of what was going on for him emotionally, and being absolutely clear about what we were going to be doing, had a huge impact on his attitude, and certainly on mine. We no longer entered into things blindly or with anxiety. I had to be the one to set up the playing field. I could no longer expect him to just figure it out, or make it up as we go, like we used to. I am comfortable flying by the seat of my pants; he is not. He needs dependable structure and positive strokes from me. Prior to mapping things out and being clear about what, when, and how we are going to do things, I think we got very little that was positive from each other.

CHANGING PERCEPTIONS CHANGES BEHAVIOR

As Einstein said, "Theory dictates what we observe." If we see our child as an out-of-control, disobedient handful, then in all probability that's what we will continue to see. And these perceptions will guide our actions and reactions toward him. However, we can choose to attend to and reinforce the moments when our children are "doing all the right stuff." This acknowledges that we are in their corner, both supporting them and cheering them on. A father said:

I used to think that, if I let my son get away with anything, he would turn out to be some kind of manipulator or bad citizen, so I rode him hard any and every time he did something I thought was inappropriate. It got to the point where I would jump on him if I even suspected he did something wrong. I found myself bracing and waiting for him to screw up. I wish I could take those times back. Since I can't, I can make a decision to treat him differently now. You know, since I have changed my attitude toward him, I have seen— we all have seen—a huge shift in his behavior.

The way we view the world around us determines the way we choose to respond to the world. Modifying the way we view things will have a direct and often immediate influence on what we do and feel. If we perceive our sons as being bad, as having mostly sharp edges, or as being too brittle so they'll break easy, they may proceed through life feeling ugly and misunderstood by family and the larger community. Our perceptions will determine how loved and prized our children feel. If our perceptions are validating, when other people don't understand them, it will be of little consequence, because our children will know the true value of their own worth. Table 7 list suggestions for changing our perspectives.

TABLE 7

How Can We Change Perspectives

◆ Know that your son is not doing things to annoy you or upset you on purpose. His lack of internal organization and impulsive approach toward things overrides rational and reasonable expectations.

◆ Know and understand what your primary reaction is toward your son when you are angry or enraged.

◆ Think about the possible alternative responses you can make instead of hitting, yelling, grabbing, verbally abusing, or emotionally withdrawing. (For example, recognize that your son's behavior is isolated and situationally specific.) With the right type of response the incident can blow over. Misguided anger can intensify the problem while making your son feel even less worthy.

◆ Know that the incident—in the larger scheme of things—is only one of millions of responses your son will make.

◆ Realize you too make mistakes, misread situations, and have the capacity to become volatile.

◆ If you find yourself becoming angry or frustrated, take a break from the situation and go for a walk, take some deep breaths, and enlist your spouse or companion for help.

◆ Envision in your mind the kind of responses to your son you want to make. (For example, "If he isn't listening or following my simple directives, this is how I will handle it.")

◆ Tell your spouse or companion how you want to respond. This establishes a "response contract."

THE ROAD LESS TRAVELED

It is natural to feel bad or guilty when we regret acting in a particular way. Guilt is largely the by-product of unfulfilled or unrealized expectations. We have expectations about what we want from others and from ourselves. We expect ourselves to act in a particular way and function at a specific level, which is in accordance with our age and our personal values. When we fall short of that mark, an internal mechanism informs us, "Hey, you really blew that one." Our thoughts and feelings team up to remind us that we are human. In the words of one father who felt guilt about his early relationship with his son who has ADHD:

My wife is a recovering alcoholic, and she has worked really hard to find both an emotional and spiritual balance in her life. Although I have an enduring respect for her now, during the early years of Brad's life, when the symptoms of ADHD had the family at each other's throats, I tended to deny my wife's drinking and Brad's cries for help. I crawled into an emotional hole and did not want to deal with what was happening. From my doing this, I think Brad has a sense that I didn't care and wasn't there for him. Part of this is true, and the other part is, how can I realistically begin showing my caring now? I frequently wonder about the emotional scars created during that time. I always feel I have to make it up to him for having abandoned him back then.

Just as experiencing guilt is a natural part of being human, so is the need to let go of that guilt in order to root ourselves in the present. We can decide what type of father we want to be right now. This is the **opportunity of fatherhood,** the ability to learn from what we have done in order to be to our children what we want and what they need. Unresolved guilt can feel like an alba-

The ship's captain does not assert his will against the forces of nature, but rather works with the forces he encounters. (page 21)

tross around our neck, hindering us from realizing the true potential of our relationships. If we remain weighed down in guilt, and continually feel we owe our children because of previous failings, it becomes almost impossible to establish clear and healthy boundaries in the relationship.

Mutually satisfying relationships are borne out of honest sharing and a willingness to forgive. An inability to forgive often signals the end of a once-meaningful relationship. A healthy relationship is one rooted in mutual respect and guided by agreed-upon boundaries and personal limits. As Riane Eisler, an Outward Bound instructor, stated, "There will always be conflict in human affairs, because of the simple fact that I'm hungry when you're thirsty, I want to sleep when you want to get up, I want to go left when you want to go right. The issue isn't conflict itself; it is how we deal with it."

Without clear limits and boundaries, a relationship exists on a bed of sand; it can be vanquished with each rising tide. Acknowledging our mistakes, to ourselves and to others, gives us permission to pursue the type of relationship we want in the present. One father captures the power of personal forgiveness:

After years of feeling just awful about the way I treated Justin, I finally realized I could start right now making meaningful changes in our relationship. Before, my treatment of him was contingent on his behavior. If he was good, I gave him my attention and time. If he was defiant, I either ignored him or berated him. It was a real conditional relationship. When things were going bad for him, I would throw salt in the wound by constantly pointing out what a disappointment he was. What was I thinking? Anyway, now I consciously accept him where he is at and work with him, rather then pull the rug out from under him when he is already off balance. This has made a dramatic difference in all of us.

Compassion and forgiveness are the cornerstones of parenting. These concepts become even more critical when we have children who feel misunderstood and often out of step with the rest of the world. Pushing beyond guilt or feelings of shame was described by a father in this manner:

I knew pretty much right away that Curtis had a problem. When he was two or three years old, he just didn't fit in with kids his same age. My wife was more reluctant to believe he was having problems. I think she was feeling guilty. It's natural to feel some type of guilt. I know I did, whether it was the origin of ADHD or the way I have treated him. I said, "Look, regardless of whose responsibility it is, the bottom line is there is no question that he has difficulties sitting still and getting along with other kids. We have to give him the support that will let him feel accepted in school and with other kids. We need to get him some help now." I encouraged her to talk with the doctors about what this could be. We already had a friend who said that it may be ADHD. We now negotiate the best way to deal with Curtis.

Changing our perspective in order to tap the natural goodness in our children is the first, and often the most difficult, step toward closeness to our children and away from guilt and anger. As stated in the *Talmud Shabbat*: "What is hateful to you, do not to others. That is the entire law; all the rest is commentary." Or, as it is expressed in the Bible: "Do unto others as you would have them do unto you." It is amazing that such a short and concise saying can capture the meaning of all the laws of God and man. Knowing our own reactions—to being yelled at, berated, humiliated—teaches us what our children experience when we lose control and saturate them with our anger and frustration.

The commitment to open our hearts to our children who have ADHD creates limitless opportunities for sharing and personal growth. A father describes his evolution from being firm-handed and distant to loving and supportive:

I think the way I spend time with him and talk to him is very respectful of where he is developmentally. It wasn't always that way, unfortunately. I used to blanket him with a lot of pressure to do things my way. Because, of course, I was the dad and the adult! He owed me because of all the things I did for him. Now, I rarely yell at him or apply emotional pressure to conform to any given situation. If I think he is going astray or stumbling a bit, we'll go play a round of golf. He likes to do that, and it gives us time alone so we can walk around and have a conversation. I give him the opportunity to discuss things with me to the extent that he is willing to tell me about his feelings or personal issues. As he is getting older, he is less inclined to share with me the way he used to. But that's OK, because I know he is moving into an age where he is more private and less willing to share. We also share a love for soccer. I help coach his team, and he sees me interacting with and influencing a lot of other kids his age. I think this has helped in his respect for me and his willingness to confide in me. Even though he is becoming more private, I believe he knows I am here and will always be here to support him and advocate for him.

Understanding the developmental stage of your child helps reduce some of the loss or resentment as he becomes more private and less in need of your presence. You can honor the developmental shift, while still offering opportunities to talk and to share. This father discovered the context best suited to engage his son in conversation and sharing. This involved knowing what interests the child. If we invite our children to join us in an activity we consider fun and they refuse or begrudgingly participate, we may feel slighted, angry, and resentful. Knowing our child's interests, along with the best times to get his attention and interact with him, can stave off a great deal of frustration.

Children with ADHD have an uncanny ability to anger even the most even-tempered person. They can be demanding, indecisive, and seemingly unappreciative. They are constantly under siege by their own biology as well as the demands levied on them by home, the community, and school. One father described the pressure this way:

Because of Tray's behavioral difficulties, he has always had the eye on him. He does not live without much scrutiny, both at home and in school. He's always the guy who finds the one thing he is not supposed to find. He'll open the drawer with the sharpest knives, or he just always gets into the wrong or inappropriate things. It seems everyone has always kept him under a giant microscope. So, as you can imagine, he is pretty self-conscious about his behavior and his attitude. You know, he is only six, so often I just want to say, "Maybe just leave him alone. Let's treat him like a normal kid, rather than a bomb ready to explode." When we see he is jumpy or having a hard time holding it together, we let him go outside to run around and just feel the freedom of being a kid. There is so much pressure on him to fit in. Before, if he were doing his homework and he started playing around and not paying attention, I would start yelling and bullying him into paying attention. I now know he just can't do what is required when he loses focus. So, we let him go find it by giving him permission to cut loose and go play.

The beneficial aspect of having children with special needs is that we are constantly afforded the opportunity to support our child in new and creative ways. Children with ADHD are extraordinarily resilient and forgiving. As one father states:

Tim has taught me a lot about myself and about forgiveness. I remember one evening that was particularly rough, because Tim's attitude and whatnot was really pissing me off. I spent a fair amount of the evening being angry and distant from him. When I went to bed that evening I was still angry, and disappointed in the way I had treated him. As I was getting ready for bed, I found on my pillow this picture he had drawn of two people, one big and one small, holding hands amidst all these trees and flowers, with the words "My dad, my friend. I am sorry." "Friend" and "sorry" were spelled wrong, and even though he didn't know how to spell or draw particularly well, he took a risk and made me the picture. It was a risk because one of the reasons I was so angry was because he just couldn't remember his spelling words. I thought he was being lazy. The picture he drew was about the two of us, together in a safe and magical place. I sat on the edge of the bed and cried. He couldn't control his behavior that evening, I could have. He didn't purposely try to hurt me, I wanted to hurt him. He showed forgiveness, I didn't. He's 8, and I am 42.

Each moment presents us with a new opportunity to be different with our children. Later in the interview, this same father referred back to the story he just told, and said the moment was a turning point for him in how he treated his son. He noted that, although it wasn't easy changing some of his perceptions or attitudes toward his son, over time and with consistent effort he was able to deal with his son's emotional difficulties much more positively.

ANGER: HOT AS VOLCANIC LAVA

Of all the emotions we experience, anger can be one of the most destructive and hurtful. Although anger is an important survival mechanism for all of us, if left unregulated it can rob us of relationships, self-esteem, and other things we hold near and dear. Anger is a warning mechanism. It warns us that something in our outside environment is infusing stress into our lives. Its cause can be a boss, the car that just cut you off, or your child with ADHD. The objective is not to eliminate anger, but rather to control it so that it does not control you. One father described getting so angry at his son that it felt like:

Hot volcanic lava was gushing up to my head. I lost all rationality. I just began spewing anger at my son to the point where he was emotionally picked clean.

Anger is an early warning sign that something or someone is causing you to jump into a defensive posture, with your shield and sword ready to strike. If we lack the necessary skills to defuse the anger, it will overrun us like an opposing army. Our children, especially our sons with ADHD, cannot withstand a full frontal assault of anger. When they are frantic and off balance, managing our anger can help them regain a foothold. One father struggled with learning to manage his anger regarding his son's ADHD:

I think it is fair to say that I have always been fairly angry. Like Mark, I had ADHD and got snubbed by just about everyone. I didn't do very well in school, so I spent most of my time with friends or playing sports. I generally felt inferior to almost everyone. I didn't talk about it much, but that's how I felt. My parents did their best to understand me, but I was a hard kid to raise.

I had an explosive temper and funneled most of my aggression through sports or high-risk activities like parachuting, hang gliding, and rock climbing. I remember being very angry growing up. I can't say exactly why, but I was. I often kept my anger inside and had this appearance to the outside world as a nice guy who was really laid back. I didn't feel very laid back. It was an act to try and fit in. I was this big "yes" man. I believe my anger and stress have really popped out since having Mark. He is a beautiful boy, but he has this side of him that cuts right through me and pulls out my anger. For a long time, I would vacillate between being overly protective and caring with him to being enraged. It was unhealthy for both of us.

One counselor I was talking to said that Mark's inability to control some of his behavior brings out a lot of unresolved anger in me because of my own problems with personal control. This made a lot of sense, but I wasn't sure what to do with it. Mark still could bring out a terrible side of me. One evening we had this bad situation where he had done something—I can't even remember what. I just lost it. I mean I felt like temporarily I lost touch with what was happening. I grabbed him, hit him, threw him down. I felt like my heart was going to push through my chest. He was cowering in the corner, with his favorite stuffed animal, looking absolutely defeated, mumbling to himself. I wanted to just die. I didn't want to ever do anything like this again.

After seeing a counselor, I finally began to see the connection between me taking the lead and him following. Before, I led with anger, and he followed. Like me, he was angry a lot, pouty, and not much fun to be with. Now that I am learning to control my anger, and talk with him about how his behavior makes me feel, he is much less moody and angry. I never had anyone show me how to use my anger constructively, or that anger is a healthy thing when it is used appropriately. My anger used to scare the crap out of me, my wife, and the kids. I feel a sense of control now. Occasionally I will still get angry, and I see Mark flinch or turn his side to me in fear. That is an automatic tip-off for me to slow things down, calm down, and let him know I am angry and what needs to happen for things to calm down. Or, if I am really angry, I pass it off to my wife until I can get a better perspective. I can say this approach is working.

◆   ◆   ◆

A TIME TO HEAL

It has become very clear in talking with the fathers of boys who have ADHD that, once a dad begins to think differently about his son's ADHD and realizes it is neither the father's nor the son's fault, the relationship can begin to break free of interaction patterns and power struggles that served to create problems.

In order to create a new, stronger relationship, the father must take the lead by introducing into the relationship a new attitude and new responses to old behaviors. As a father changes and the son feels the attitude change is "for real" and will last, the son's behavior will be marked by fewer problems, and those that do occur will be shorter in duration. We cannot expect our sons to change on their own. A shift in our perspective, attitude, and behavior regarding ADHD can be the catalyst needed to bring about emotional and relationship change.

ADHD elicits strong feelings and emotions from parents, teachers, and peers. It is sometimes helpful to think about the onset of ADHD-related problem behaviors as similar to an earthquake, which develops quickly and often unexpectedly. In the aftermath of the earthquake, the degree of damage is dependent on the degree to which the underlying fault lines shifted. The more intense the shift, the more devastating are the consequences. People have a range of responses in preparing for earthquakes. Some design their homes with added support and stronger foundations to withstand even the most intense shock. This seems to minimize the impact of the quake. Others give preparation barely a thought, believing, "It's going to happen, so what can I really do about it?" These people generally experience a greater loss and trauma when the quake hits.

The emotions brought about by ADHD can feel like a shock to the system. Preparing for it—by knowing it is often unintentional on your child's part, having the support of a spouse or companion, and consciously knowing how you will respond—can significantly lessen the jolt and the accompanying pain. Learning how to prepare for the shock and its aftermath is a process that often takes time and a great deal of reflection.

Barry was two and a half when I started to become frustrated with him. He was constantly on the move and did not seem to hear or understand the word "no." It was more than the "terrible twos," it was just flat-out terrible. I started feeling stressed-out and generally pissed off at him. It was also increasing the friction between me and my wife.

My mother said to me one day, "You know, in a lot of ways that is how I remember you being when you were young." That is seriously the last thing I wanted to hear. Growing up for me was not easy, and I had these visions of it being different for my son. As I thought more about it, and as more frustration developed, I realized that if I had a problem when I was young, Jamie may have the same problem.

He is now eight, and I see many of the characteristics in him that I wanted to have him avoid—like low self-esteem or seeing himself as bad. Sometimes no matter how hard my wife and I try, we can't protect him from the world, and the world's reflection of how it sees him. He's old enough to see his reflection in what he does and the attitudes he conveys. This reflection must be difficult to deal with sometimes. He says things like, "I am stupid" or "I must be retarded, because all the other kids in class don't have problems in school." He is now aware of his struggles, and it's hard to see him go through this, because he wants so bad to be good.

If we envision parenting our child with ADHD as a personal challenge rather than a burden, we enter into a realm of limitless possibilities. Doing this requires a paradox of sorts: In order to bring our child closer to us and to himself, we must loosen our own tightly held grip on fear or anger. Fear and anger can create two extremes to parenting a child with ADHD. We can be either overly controlling and overly punitive, or we can be aloof and distant, leaving the bulk of the parenting to someone else. When we are afraid, it is difficult to view something as a challenge. Fear tends to keep us anchored in primitive survival-type responses—screaming, yelling, grabbing, and hitting. Seeing a given situation as a challenge keeps us focused on winning and achieving, precisely those accomplishments that we want for our sons—to be winners and achievers in accordance with their abilities. Some ideas for increasing success by supporting your son are listed in Table 8.

TABLE 8

Increasing Success Through Support

◆ Highlight your caring for and belief in your son. This requires paying attention to "the small stuff" and magnifying it so he feels empowered.

◆ Encourage your son to participate in finding solutions to a problem. This makes him feel his voice and opinion matter.

◆ When trouble develops, calmly remove your son from the situation and discuss options and possible solutions. Highlight the necessity for both give and take in any relationship.

◆ Admit when you are wrong! This is fundamental in helping your son understand that we all make mistakes and what to do about them. (For example "I am sorry for hitting you for your behavior. I became very angry and lost my temper. I was wrong, and I will try my hardest to deal with my anger in a better way.")

◆ Keep consequences simple and appropriate. Putting your son in his room for half the day because he blurted out an inappropriate word will make him feel hopeless about redeeming himself. Give him a parachute whenever possible.

A challenge can bring out the best in us and result in big rewards. As a father of a nine-year-old boy said:

What I am doing right now is trying to prepare Pete for when he enters junior high school and is confronted with some tough choices. You know, like girls, drugs, etc. I look at this as a real challenge. The outcome will be more evident in a few years when he has to deal with these issues. I feel the time I spend with him is setting him up to make solid and responsible choices when he gets older. Since I spent very little time with my father, I can already see the value of the time Pete and I spend together. I am very involved in his personal development and try to support him in the decisions that he makes. Even if it is not a terribly positive decision, we take the time to discuss how he would do it differently next time. I think this approach, and being respectful of what he is capable of doing, is paying big dividends. Even though he has ADHD, I can see at a young age that he is developing a solid morality and understands what constitutes good choices and bad choices. I think there are times we all make poor or less-than-ideal choices; the key is what we do the next time we are in the same situation.

Chapter 4

HOW ADHD AFFECTS FAMILIES

Children with ADHD can cause a great deal of tension within the marriage and the family. Raising a child with ADHD requires a lot of communication and discussion between the parents. Very little can be taken for granted. It seems that the more parents talk and share their feelings, the less tension invades the relationship.

MARITAL STRESS

If parents have drastically different parenting styles, and remain rigid or stuck in their preferred style, the relationship can be in trouble. When parents are out of sync with one another, the marital relationship can feel burdensome. Perhaps this is one of the contributing factors to the increased rate of divorce in families with children who have ADHD.

My wife seems much more patient, or should I say tolerant, of some of Aaron's behavior. I just won't tolerate it. After a while I lose patience, and just want him to snap out of it and get it together. My wife doesn't remain angry at Aaron for very long. It's kind of like, I'm pissed and now it's over. I tend to hold on to the anger. This really makes her mad, then she is mad at me and we are in this pool of tension. I know she is right, but I find it hard letting go of some of his behavior and negative attitude. I resent it. I resent that he can't be more respectful or balanced. I just resent it. So I guess I have a tantrum to demonstrate my anger. This makes things worse, and definitely makes things strained in the marriage.

Children who observe parental discord may develop a divide-and-conquer attitude that contributes to family tension and marital conflict. More positive outcomes occur when parents collaborate and support one another in developing effective parenting strategies.

My wife tends to be a threatener and I spank. She tends not to follow through on her threats and I tend not to give many warnings or have many discussions. Both methods cause us problems. I want her to follow through and she wants me to talk more and give them more options. Often the focus of the problem will go from something the boys did to us fighting about how we did or didn't handle the situation. It's ridiculous. She has her approach and I have mine. It is clear when we collaborate with the boys, things go much smoother and better.

The recognition that a spouse has a different parenting philosophy or a lower threshold for negative behavior can cause marital strife if nothing is done to accommodate each spouse's needs. In the following example, a father describes having a much higher tolerance for the negative behaviors associated with ADHD. The wife, on the other hand, finds the social display of negative behaviors very troubling. The different styles will result in marital tension without an agreed-upon plan of communication and action.

Here is a great story. A friend of mine and I took the kids out to West Virginia, to this outlet mall. Dennis was having a huge temper tantrum in the mall. We're coming up the steps, and this girl is staring at us, looking at us, looking at Dennis in disbelief. I look right at her and say, "And he's my nice kid." That's how I'll deal with it. My wife, of course, will want to get in the car and drive right home. She'd be mortified. It causes tension when we are together and things start going bad for Dennis. She'll be stressing out and upset, and I'll be trying to blow it off. This just makes her more furious because I am not supporting her and helping to reduce the stress.

An effective interaction between parents involves one parent being able to take over when the other is experiencing extreme stress. As in any family, there will inevitably be moments of stress, but the family with a child who has ADHD experiences those moments more often. Knowing when to let the other parent step in can relieve the tension and maintain open lines of communication.

My wife would get pretty stressed out about Rob's behavior. So I frequently would step in and try to be the voice of reason, to try and get Rob out of the situation so things could calm down. I think my wife has appreciated the times I step in to help relieve some of the tension.

Everyone's always kept him under a
giant microscope. (page 47)

Recognizing and supporting one another's parenting strengths
can help minimize marital disruption stemming from ADHD.
The following describes a fathers's recognition that his wife has
a better sense of his son's emotional needs because she interacts
with him more regularly. He found deferring to her expertise
beneficial for both their child and their relationship.

I'd say Ben takes more advantage of my wife than he does
of me. I also think she is in a position to know him better
and know how to handle him. She sees him more frequently

than I do, so she would be the one he would try to have bend the rules or test. I defer to her a lot when he is having problems. It may not always be what I would have done, but it is not worth a fight between us. I generally follow her lead. This keeps things fairly well-balanced.

Marital conflict develops when husbands and wives have different and contradictory styles of disciplining. Children with ADHD can create such emotional upheaval that the parents begin arguing about the most effective methods of discipline. Finding an agreed-upon approach often allows the parents to be mutually supportive, even when emotions are running high.

It's fair to say that our marriage has been strained due to Brian's ADHD. I have one style of dealing with his disruptive behavior and my wife has another way of dealing with it. If I am yelling or upset, it feels to me like she rescues him from the consequence of his actions. This incites me even more, and I begin then getting mad at her. It is a process of finding a balance between the two of us. I think we certainly try to talk about the best approach to parenting Brian. There is a part of me that is resentful toward Brian for creating tension between my wife and me. I think she tends to be too much of a pushover most of the time. After it builds up and she can't tolerate it anymore, then she erupts. I then come to Brian's aid when she is upset. We keep trying to find a balance where his behavior will not pit us against each other.

Mutual acceptance of the presence of ADHD is a necessary precondition for developing a suitable parenting strategy. If one parent does not accept the ADHD diagnosis, it can be very difficult to establish an agreed-upon parenting method.

The following scenario forecasts the type of outcome that is possible when a husband and wife are seen by their children as a "united front" and is a wonderful description of what happens during times of parental consensus. Clearly this togetherness can prevent the emotional tension from moving from the child to the parental unit.

◆ ◆ ◆

My wife and I try not to override each other. There will be a time where she's just had a real rough day; perhaps it's because she had the night shift and she didn't get much sleep and Troy comes home and he had a bad day on the playground. He starts spilling juice and getting under her skin. She's at the end of her rope. I walk in the door and I've been at work all day and I want to see my family, and there is absolute chaos. Since I haven't had to deal with it all day, I can step in with a more objective fresh approach and bail her out. She'll want to banish him to his room forever, while I'll sit down with him for a minute and just keep an eye on him and try to get him focused on something. This works real well. It creates less tension, my wife feels supported, and Troy isn't in the doghouse. She is also able to help me in the same way. It is a nice working partnership. We need this with a guy as active and all over the place as Troy.

◆ ◆ ◆

Knowing when to assist, or when to ask for assistance from the other parent, helps reduce tension and preserve a balance. Parental consistency and agreement on disciplining strategies have a positive effect on the couple's relationship independent of the benefit for the son. This father suggests that the couple's current level of unity evolved over time. It took quite a bit of trial and error to achieve the balance they currently enjoy.

◆ ◆ ◆

Both of us have definitely improved in the way we deal with Ricky. I think we recognize the problems inherent in what we had done previously in trying to deal with his problems. I think one of the lessons we have learned in raising Ricky is that we have to be more consistent about how we are going to handle his behavior and how we intend to follow through with sanctions.

◆ ◆ ◆

TABLE 9

Strengthening the Marital Unit

◆ Remember that your spouse's and your style of disciplining are a function of or reaction to the type of discipline you received as a child and may be different.

◆ Be clear about your natural disciplining style. Recognize that it will probably be different from that of your spouse. If it is different, understand how it is different.

◆ Try at all costs to agree upon a discipline plan with your spouse. Marital discord is a common by-product of ADHD when spouses have different discipline strategies.

◆ Minimize power struggles by acknowledging the feelings of your spouse.

◆ Make a verbal or written contract with one another that when something difficult arises, you will both take time to consider the most appropriate action. This serves to slow the situation down and promote a more meaningful partnership.

◆ When appropriate, you can both leave the situation to discuss what to do. This again reduces emotion, shows a united front, and allows you to be more flexible and less rigid when problems develop.

There are many ways to strengthen the marital unit and elicit spousal support. A few of these can be found in Table 9.

FAMILY STRUCTURE

It is important that the mother and father act as the "executive branch" of the family. Children should be allowed their say, but the bottom line rests with the parents. At times, it is possible for parents to feel completely dominated by the behaviors stemming from ADHD. They no longer feel in control of their families or their children. The following two families offer some important guidelines for parents to maintain their executive power:

Our kids do not run our home. What we do is considered by all, but the bottom line rests with my wife and me. The children know the structure of our family and how things run. We try to create as much of a predictable environment as possible. When they get home from school, they can go out and play for a while. We try to eat dinner when I am home at a certain time. My wife helps with their homework pretty much at a certain time. We want to know where they are going and where they are. Bedtime is usually set at the same time during the weekdays. Saturday morning they can sleep as late as they want.

They are not allowed to fly all over the neighborhood, over to the mall, or over to a friend's house. And while they are involved in many activities, we don't let them get involved in whatever they want. What they do outside the home is heavily considered. This type of structure works well for all the children, especially Pat, who starts to fray a little bit if things become unstructured.

♦ ♦ ♦

Without a doubt, Allen has to see us in charge. We can't have the tail wagging the dog. We run the house, and that is exactly what he must see. If Allen or the other two begin running the house, we've got the clowns running the circus. Allen knows when we say something we mean it. If he chooses not to do it, then it will cost him an activity he wants to do. We frame things out in the family in terms of "choices." "You have a choice. Do this now or it will run into your TV time," or whatever. Even if Allen is having a real problem controlling himself, we say that it is obvious it is too difficult for him to be with us right now, he must leave the room and go to his room or some other place in the house where he can gain some control. Being consistent is also an important part of this.

Building a workable family structure around the emotional needs of a child with ADHD reduces family stress while increasing the functional level of the child. This does not imply that the child with ADHD runs the family or determines the structure; rather, it means that the parents are aware of potential problems and adjust the family structure to avoid emotional or behavioral pitfalls.

◆   ◆   ◆

We are not rigid with the way we deal with Philip. We try to recognize where he is at emotionally and meet his needs. It is easy for us to lose sight of the fact that he has a medical problem. When we start imposing unrealistic structures on him, it becomes self-defeating. We pay attention to him, and allow him to show us, by his behavior and emotions, how to best deal with a particular situation. What's right for us or what makes sense to us may not line up with Philip's immediate disposition.

◆   ◆   ◆

WORKING PARENTS

In a two-parent household where both work, there is an enormous amount of pressure to get ready and out of the door every morning. This type of harried existence has an impact not only on the parents, but on the child as well. Such routines can create a great deal of stress. Parents must figure out what types of rituals increase or decrease stress. Daily schedules have a big effect on parenting a child who has ADHD.

> Let me give you an example of what life is like in our family. We had a psychologist who looked at Les and asked the big question, "Does he dress himself?" One of the things that happens in our household is that my wife works nights at a hospital, three days a week. In the morning I give the kids a bath. I get them dressed, and I take care of my own morning ritual to prepare for the day. In about an hour's time, I've got to get three people bathed and dressed. I don't have time to sit with Les and show him how to put his shirt on, how to put his pants on. He just has to be dressed in five minutes. The psychologist's question was one of the benchmarks. It was a terrible question because, yeah, I think he knows how to dress himself. I've seen him take off his shirt. I've seen him put his underwear on. But in the morning, to get dressed in five minutes, I've got to dress him.

In order to relieve some of the stresses felt in that rush each morning, it is important for families to develop a plan or strategy. Table 10 offers some suggestions to make morning routines easier.

The presence or absence of the father affects the emotional climate of the child with ADHD, as well as general family functioning. The father below has very little idea of how the family operates or the particular struggles that his son faces. He seems to connect his work-related unavailability to the son's feelings of anger and hostility. It is also clear that his wife has the responsibility of coordinating almost everything related to family logistics and structure:

TABLE 10

Relaxing Morning Routines

◆ Decide who will be in charge of the morning routine or of different steps involved in getting out of the house. For example, Dad will supervise dressing, brushing teeth, and medication; Mom will be responsible for breakfast and carpool. Make sure your children understand what needs to be accomplished each morning.

◆ Write up a morning schedule and post it where all can see it. Have your son participate in writing the schedule. Use pictures for children who cannot yet read.

◆ Practice how long it will take to complete each task. You can use a timer to move things along in the morning. Be creative. Some families have recorded their morning schedule on tape with various songs as accompaniment (for example, everyone should be down to breakfast by the time the march is playing).

◆ Prepare as much as you can the night before. Make lunches, check bookbags to make sure everything is packed, choose the clothes both you and your children will wear the next day. Taking a bath or shower the night before can save time in the morning.

◆ Have a designated spot for all items that need to be taken with you in the morning (briefcases, bookbags, lunches, musical instruments, gym clothes, etc.). This could be a large box located next to the front door. Items should be placed there each night before you go to bed.

I suppose it is fair to say that our house tends to be less stable and more chaotic. I am not home much. My job keeps me very busy and away quite a bit. Consequently, I am not as confident about what Matt is going through or the kind of problems he is having. I really rely on my wife to carry the day in that regard. I kind of make this cameo appearance every now and then. Matt is a bright kid, very charismatic, but he carries around a lot of anger and hostility. I am sure it has to do with my work hours, and partially the school frustration he must feel.

When fathers are actively involved with their sons and demonstrate consistent nurturing and caring, the sons seem to excel in their social, academic, and family performance. Involved fathers boost their children's self-esteem and self-confidence. They have the capacity to lessen many of the negative effects associated with ADHD. Positive aspects of fathers' involvement are listed in Table 11.

DIVORCE

Children with ADHD often have difficult temperaments and are difficult to soothe, so members of the family find themselves emotionally embroiled. Issues related to ADHD can became flash points in the marital relationship. Resolving these issues can be an opportunity for parents to work closer and more collaboratively. While ADHD issues may strain the fabric of a marriage, they don't need to tear it.

However, if a couple does decide on divorce to deal with the emotional stress and strain of their relationship, it is inappropriate to assume that the conflict about ADHD was the principal cause of the breakup. If divorce does occur, keep in mind that the parenting relationship will continue. Although the

TABLE 11

Impact of Fathers' Involvement

◆ An on-going commitment by the father signals to the child a sense of his own worth, irrespective of ADHD-related difficulties.

◆ A father's caring acts as an anchor for a child and allows him to put ADHD-related behaviors in perspective.

◆ With a father's guidance and belief in him, a child *feels* that the ADHD related behaviors are not insurmountable.

◆ A father can model for the child appropriate ways to channel and resolve the anger and frustration that naturally accompany ADHD.

◆ When a child feels valued, this feeling is reflected in his behavior, his attitude, and the choices he makes.

marital relationship has ended, parents must still work together to effectively manage their difficult child.

Parents must be willing to work together and improve their interaction and communication skills even after the marriage has ended. Often this involves change and the need to try something different. Even if a proposed technique is not what you would choose, listen and be open to suggestions of what works. But no matter what program is decided upon, consistency is essential. The issue is not your ex-partner being controlling but what is best for your child.

Since the custodial parent will have the child most of the time, that parent may need extra support and encouragement. Seeking out support groups or family counseling sessions may be useful. Adequate time away from family responsibilities and private time to yourself is vital and necessary. It is important not to complain about what you feel the other parent is doing wrong. Words of encouragement or shared positive experiences are always more uplifting. A parent should also never speak to the child about the ex-spouse and how he or she is perceived as handling situations. Blaming the other parent for the way the child acts or for the divorce is also counterproductive.

What can a parent do to ensure a smoother transition or improved relationship? All children, but especially children with ADHD, need consistency and structure. Maintaining as much of the same routine in both homes as possible is most helpful for smooth transitions and good behavioral responses. Bedtime, chores, and homework rituals should be kept as similar as possible. Behavioral programs should be agreed upon and set up to be consistently reinforced no matter what the environment. Promises and regular visitation schedules should be adhered to except under extreme circumstances. This should include pick-up and return times, with calls made to notify the child of any changes if complications arise. If you are the noncustodial parent, contact with your child should be frequent, regular, expected, and a positive experience for all. Table 12 lists ideas for managing divorce.

EXTENDED FAMILY

The extended family's understanding and education about ADHD have a direct impact on both the child and the family. If members of the extended family blame the child for ADHD-related behaviors, the child can easily feel shame and a sense of isolation. If extended family are not educated (or choose not to become so) about ADHD, the child can be a "scapegoat" and

TABLE 12

Managing Divorce

Realize that:

◆ Less expressed anger or hostility toward your former spouse equals a greater sense of emotional safety for your son and other children.

◆ Even though you are no longer connected by marriage, you are and always will be connected to one another as parents. This requires an ability to work together for the benefit of the children. Agreeing that your aim is to benefit the children may help in working as a constructive parental unit.

◆ Children with ADHD who are part of or witness parents' verbally assailing one another are prone to have more intense and more frequent verbal and behavioral outbursts. Displaying appropriate problem-solving strategies can definitely help reduce inappropriate ADHD-related behaviors.

◆ Contact between both parents needs to be as frequent, regular, expected, and positive as possible. Remember, your children are mourning the loss of the only parental unit they have known.

◆ Agree to keep the relationship with your former spouse separate from that with your children. If your child has a complaint or negative comment about your former spouse, encourage your child to bring up the problem with his mother. Acknowledge his feelings, and direct him back to his mother to work it out.

held responsible for negative incidents, regardless of whether he was actually involved.

I feel as a nuclear family we have been dealing with Mark's ADHD really well. He feels supported and positive. Every day is a new day and a new way for us to learn and improve on our interaction and way of dealing with Mark. I don't feel like we are headed down a tunnel with no light at the end. The greatest difficulty is my wife's family, especially her sister. Her sister's oldest child is Mark's age. Mark is the object of quite a bit of criticism in terms of his behavior. My wife used to be able to go on vacation, home for a month every summer. She loved it when her sister would come up as well. Over the years my wife would come back more agitated at the way Mark was treated and problems that developed while she was at the vacation home. Now my wife doesn't go to the vacation home—and only rarely talks to her family. She felt Mark was the object of constant criticism and negative remarks. She felt he was frequently blamed for things that he had no part of. She feels it is better for everyone, especially Mark, if the contact with her family is kept to a minimum. This is particularly sad because both my parents are deceased, and those are the only remaining grandparents that Mark has.

In comparison to the above family, the following describes one where understanding, open communication, and education about ADHD guide family interaction:

My family has never treated Trevor any differently since they learned of the ADHD. We told them everything about the ADHD and the effect it has on Trevor, especially when he is not on medication. Of course, they don't like that he is medicated, but we have explained the reasons for the medicine, and they will support whatever we do. They notice he is calmer and even more so when he is medicated. That helps in his relationship with everyone, not just his grandparents.

SIBLINGS

Within families, no two children are the same. While this uniqueness can be intellectually acknowledged, it is sometimes difficult when there is a drastic personality difference between non-ADHD siblings and the child with ADHD.

A parent may have more in common with or enjoy the personality of a non-ADHD child more than a child with ADHD. When this occurs, there can be a natural desire by the father to spend more time and develop a closer relationship with the non-ADHD child. Non-ADHD siblings may be more easygoing, more capable academically or athletically, and more socially interactive and successful. This can add to the burden that a child with ADHD must bear.

In addition, family relationships can be further complicated by intense and combative sibling jealousy. These sibling problems, commingled with a father's lack of enjoyment in being around the child with ADHD, can have a devastating influence on the afflicted child's self-worth, on family cohesiveness, and on the overall family structure.

♦ ♦ ♦

There is a pretty big gap between our two boys. Devin was born when the older one, Greg, was about five. It was pretty much intentional in that we thought by the time that Greg was four or five he would have established his identity and a feeling of attachment and importance in the family. This has turned out to be a disaster. There were absolutely no benefits and loads of problems that developed when Devin was born. Not from the very beginning, but from when the younger one was nine months and started to crawl and make his presence felt, the trouble began. Greg was just miserable to his younger brother. This was also the time that we were having Greg tested for ADHD. Even though Devin and I have similar personalities, and I really enjoy spending time with him, I find a lot of time is taken up dealing with Greg and his varied problems either at school or at home. He is a tough kid who doesn't necessarily bring out the best in me. Our home life tends to be fairly contentious and argumentative.

Sibling jealousy and a parent's preference for one child over another are critical issues that must be addressed in the family. One father dealt with this by taking a very direct approach with his son who had ADHD:

Even before my wife said anything about it, I was aware that I enjoyed and gravitated more toward spending time with my other two children—one of whom is also ADHD but has a very dynamic and fun personality. Kevin, my other ADHD son, has a very abrasive and unsettled manner—hard to please, I guess. Quite frankly, it is generally not that enjoyable for me to be around him. He knows it because I have essentially told him how I feel. Not in a mean or biting way, but I said, "Listen, I want to have fun with you and enjoy our time together, but when you have this attitude or act this way it is hard for me to be there." I also got this video from my wife that showed five different kids playing or in different situations. All had different attitudes—from pleasant to abrasive. I sat down and watched it with Kevin. I asked him who he liked the best? He pointed to the friendliest kid in the video. I said, "You know, I liked him the best, too. That's how I want to get along with you." The boy's name in the video was Sal. So now, when things are tense between us, I'll kind of jokingly say, "Hey, remember

Sal. What would he do?" I have to say that things have been better. Our good times seem to be building on themselves.

◆ ◆ ◆

Being direct with our children is different from being blunt or saying things that will knowingly hurt their feelings. Being direct entails developing an environment within which our children can learn. In many ways it involves setting the stage with all the props and necessary lighting to create the effect we want. This approach, of course, requires energy and time. The father in the above scenario used a video as a critical prop in setting the learning stage. This let the child know he was worth the time, effort, and honesty set forth by the father. It is far easier to dismiss our children then to display the caring and affection described above.

When siblings engage in destructive fighting patterns or the non-ADHD sibling has developed the habit of scapegoating the child with ADHD, parental intervention is needed to create a sense of balance and family harmony. In many ways parents need to act as alter egos for their children when negative interaction sequences dominate the sibling relationship. Setting a standard for conflict resolution and having this standard modeled by the parents teaches siblings how feelings and disagreements will be handled in the family and the consequences when this standard is violated.

One method many parents use is to educate the whole family about ADHD and its impact. This can be accomplished by attending local support groups, reading books, or obtaining some form of family counseling. In this way, siblings can learn that many of the ADHD-related behaviors are not intentional or immediately within the control of the child. The child with ADHD also learns about the impact of his behavior or attitude on family members.

Table 13 offers ways to encourage better sibling relationships.

TABLE 13

Encouraging Positive Sibling Relationships

◆ The way you feel about, describe, and treat your son with ADHD will inform his siblings how to treat him. Your behavior will be used as the model.

◆ Resist comparing your son with ADHD to non-ADHD siblings or peers. This can be very degrading and set a standard in the family that condones putting down the child with ADHD.

◆ When a sibling has a problem with the child who has ADHD, encourage the siblings to work out the problem in a peaceful manner. You can discuss the problem with both of them, find out how each contributed to the problem, and discuss with them what type of solution would work best. Each child must understand how the actions of the other affected them. This builds empathy.

◆ Point out each child's strengths. There is a tendency to praise the child with ADHD less then his non-ADHD siblings. This can set a negative standard.

◆ If you decide to place your son with ADHD on a behavior management program, place all your children on a similar program. All children can afford to improve certain behaviors. This creates a positive environment for all the children.

◆ Try to spend Special Time alone with each of your children. Whether it is going out to lunch, a walk in the woods, a one-on-one basketball game, or watching a tape together. This separates the children and allows a special relationship with you to develop with each of them.

FAMILY MEETINGS

The following describes a simple method one family uses to address overall family issues:

Once a week, lately it has been on Wednesday evenings, we have a family council meeting. The meeting is structured to deal with the range of family situations and issues we are all involved in. It is not solely focused on the negative. It can be updates, preparation for vacation, or redesigning family chores and responsibilities. It's not meant to be a bitch session. Each week, a different family member chairs the meeting and is responsible for watching the time and making sure everyone who wants to speak has a chance. Everyone must give a brief update on how they are doing and say at least one thing they like about what they are doing. Unresolved arguments are dealt with in the council, and we often do role playing to resolve issues. For instance, if my wife and I are in a dispute about something, two of the children will play our roles, the way we are currently acting, and a way that would be more productive. The session ends by each of us saying one thing we appreciate about the other people in the family. This has been a saving grace for our family in many ways.

This family consistently and creatively makes the time and expends the effort to remain connected. In a fast-paced society, with increased demands on our time and on our minds, devoting this kind of time consistently requires discipline and belief in the process. The focus is not solely on problems or the ADHD child as the problem; the focus is on family functioning and working productively as a unit.

The example above teaches us not to overfocus on the problem, but rather to involve the whole family in a process of positive interaction and constructive problem solving. Telling the kids that they are not allowed to fight, or that the child with ADHD is responsible for the problem, will only serve to heighten aggression and tension in the family.

"And he's my nice kid." (page 57)

Another method for resolving sibling disputes is to require the disputing siblings to sit in a specific place in the house and stay there until they talk through the problem and hear each other's side of the story. A parent generally needs to be involved in this process initially in order to teach the children how to listen without interrupting, how to take turns, and what it means to resolve a problem. This type of strategy is helpful when one or more of the children become overly aggressive or abusive toward one another. It is important that the parent remain calm during this interaction, and that the siblings cannot get up and leave until they jointly agree to discontinue the negative or problematic interaction. Again, with only a little focus on the problem and a concerted family effort directed toward a solution, improved relationships can be the result.

Chapter 5

MANAGING ADHD: DISCIPLINE

◆ ◆ ◆

My wife is really concerned about our son's moral discipline, and rightfully so. I'm more concerned about the discipline in life, of putting things in place, of making sure that you understand where something is because you will need it later, of knowing what you are responsible for. I think it is essential to understand the consequence of our actions, great or small. I think that a personal discipline about following through, and delaying gratification of something, precedes the development of a moral discipline. I think Bart would be hard-pressed to show respect for another if he hasn't learned to slow down enough to initiate doing and completing his homework or respecting the value of money and material things. Without this, moral discipline would be almost impossible to achieve. If Bart learns personal discipline, then the moral discipline will naturally evolve from our modeling and the values we live in the family.

—Father of a seven-year-old boy

◆ ◆ ◆

WHAT DO YOU MEAN BY "DISCIPLINE"?

Walk into any public arena—a mall, circus, sporting event, restaurant—where children and their parents interact and you will probably see it. At least one family is in crisis. The child has exhibited no self-control, and nothing the parents do seems to have an effect. Your first reaction may be to consider the child "undisciplined"—and certainly the kid's actions fit our conventional definition. However, if you look closely, there's probably another element to the interaction. Ask whether the parents are exhibiting any "discipline" of their own. Are they remaining calm, consistent, and supportive throughout the undeniably stressful exchange? Or are they surrendering as much self-control as the child, and reacting with an equal amount of anger and abandon?

When we use the term "discipline," we are referring to two specific forms of interaction with our children: one, our emotional response to their negative attitudes and behaviors, the other, the behavior management strategies we employ, either to initiate behaviors we want or to stop behaviors we don't want. In this chapter we will focus on our emotional response to our children's attitudes and behaviors. The next chapter will examine behavior management strategies in greater depth.

What is the connection between disciplining a child and a child's learning self-discipline? There is a direct link between the way children are disciplined and the degree to which they assume responsibility for their own actions and behaviors.

Disciplining a child, especially a child with ADHD, is complicated by our own emotional response to what we consider misbehaving or other social improprieties. The more emotionally consumed we become by our children's behavior, the more likely we are to utilize ineffective or inappropriate disciplining strategies, such as hitting, screaming, threatening, bullying, or withdrawing love and attention. When we lead with our emotions, the outcome is usually less then desirable, and often regrettable.

How we choose to discipline our children is one of the most fundamental aspects of raising a child with ADHD. As noted by one father:

◆ ◆ ◆

I used to be a lot stricter with him. I'd treat him like a normal kid, meaning that I really didn't take into account that he had difficulty processing information or following rules. I would keep harping on him and trying to make him act like any other kid his age. I've come to learn that is not him, that he is not like many of his friends. In some ways he is more in control. I attribute that to the work we have been doing to create more consistency in our home, and definitely to reduce getting too emotionally attached to the issue. It is not that he doesn't want to do things, it is just that he can't always do it the way others expect or want.

◆ ◆ ◆

An essential aspect of learning how to discipline your son effectively is understanding what he is personally capable of doing and when he is most able to do it. A child with ADHD needs his father to lean on during times when he cannot hold it together himself. If you are angry, upset, or out of control as a result of your son's behavior, you cannot provide the type of emotional support and discipline necessary to resolve the problem.

A child with ADHD needing his father's support is much like a person with a broken foot needing a crutch. He will not need to use the crutch permanently; however, in order to feel comfortable and go about his daily duties, he needs the broken foot and the crutch to work together to minimize discomfort. As the child with ADHD matures, he will need his father less for support, and more as an important sounding board and resource.

Imagine a father and son on a wilderness expedition, far from civilization and help. Because of a strange twist of fate, both are injured in an accident. Neither can go for help or utilize the emergency plan they had developed before venturing out on their journey. They are trapped in a situation where neither is in control and neither can seek help. This situation is similar to that when a father becomes emotionally unavailable and the child is not able to maintain control.

One father describes reducing his emotional response to his son's level of behavior:

I have had to learn what Matt can and can't do. I don't mean like baseball or schoolwork—I mean what he can, and sometimes can't, handle emotionally. He gets into these very weird moods where it's hard to like him sometimes. He is demanding, angry, he says mean things, and he is just very disagreeable. I used to scream and grab him when he would act like this. Without question, my response to him made things worse. I acted as inappropriately as he did in many ways. This didn't allow him to learn how to control his own behavior. During this time there was no real discipline to speak of. I just became angry that he wouldn't cooperate. I remember relying on a lot of threatening. The atmosphere wasn't there for him to learn how to control himself. Today, I now deal with him very lovingly and calmly when he gets upset. Also, I point out what he needs to do and that we are here to support him when he is ready to work with us.

CALM DISCIPLINE

The practice of remaining calm with our sons who have ADHD and establishing effective methods of discipline are fraternal twins. Remaining calm and consistently disciplining inappropriate behavior results in a child who understands and takes responsibility for his own actions and behaviors.

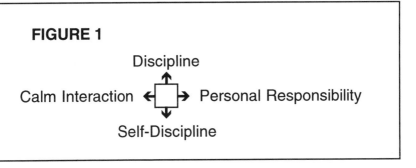

FIGURE 1

Discipline

Calm Interaction ←☐→ Personal Responsibility

Self-Discipline

If you remove any of the components from the diagram in Figure 1, it becomes incomplete and broken. The interaction of the various components lends the support necessary for dealing with many of the symptoms associated with ADHD. One of the greatest acts of love we can offer our sons who have ADHD is to remain calm in the midst of their emotional storm. This does not mean remaining placid or passive. On the contrary, it means being there with your son as he struggles to quell his internal noise. It means acknowledging how hard it must be for him to hold it together. It means being clear with him about your love and the opportunities you are offering to help him correct his emotional tailspin. A father of a nine-year-old boy gives a clear example of this:

I don't think the way I deal with Marty now at all resembles the way I used to treat him. I used to think he was just a spoiled little kid who wouldn't stop until he got his way. If he didn't get his way, he would say stuff like, "I hate you," or mumble derogatory comments under his breath. I would literally chase him up the stairs and around the house just so I could scream in his face.

I think after he was diagnosed with ADHD and we put him on medication, I believed he was going to stop a lot of the bullshit behavior that would drive me and my wife nuts. At that time, I didn't realize that a change in him hinged on a change in us. Especially in me, because my wife was much more tolerant and forgiving of his behavior. The fact that he was on medication and still acting out made me even angrier.

I didn't know how to make him act like he was supposed to. Even though my wife said I needed to look at how I reacted to Pete, it had very little effect on how I treated him. Believe it or not, things began to change for me after I read an article on disciplining your child. It was my wife's magazine, and one morning I was flipping through it and saw the article. After reading it, I was shocked at how I basically did everything to ensure that Pete *not* develop self-control and self-discipline. The screaming and punishment tactics I used made him feel even more helpless and out of control.

Shortly after this, I read another article about ADHD. It helped me understand what is going on inside of Pete's mind and body. I suppose I became more sensitive to what he was going through. I began doing more reading about how to help him when he was out of control. I rarely yell anymore. I let him know what is expected of him and what needs to happen in order for him to do what he wants. I think my not yelling and being on an even keel with him has had a huge impact on him. I see him as being much more responsible and listening much better.

This was the gist of the article: Don't get excited when your child does, be clear about expectations, be clear about family rules, and be clear about what the family limits are regarding certain behaviors and choices. The most counterproductive thing you can do is scream or hit the kid. This definitely makes the kid shrink from taking responsibility for what he did.

Modeling discipline to our children encourages them to assume mounting levels of self-discipline in dealing with their emotions and the world around them. A child visually sees, and physically feels, the healing power present when a father remains calm and supportive—even though the child feels far from that himself.

This is not easy when you consider that ADHD is a disorder affecting attention and emotion. The child's emotional regulatory system is "out of whack." Although he wants to control himself, he physically cannot. Children have described the feeling of losing control as being like having an out-of-body experience. They see the negative behavior or inattention happening but feel powerless to control it. By observing the parent exercising self-control and staying calm during those moments, the child with ADHD can begin to internalize more appropriate behavior.

RESILIENCY

Children with ADHD are incredibly resilient, resourceful, and determined. Even in the face of disappointed parents and disillusioned teachers, these kids try to hang on and "do better next time." Children who do not receive the support, empathy, and care that they need will eventually break under the weight of years of negative criticism and failed attempts at improvement. One father described his son's desire to please and do well:

I know Bret wants to control himself and fit in. I can just tell. But once things start going bad for him, he becomes more frustrated and has even a harder time. He doesn't give up, though. I know he is trying to pull things back on track. And he knows I am supporting him in doing his best at the moment. I sometimes think of myself as his "emotional air bag." I know the way I deal with him makes him feel safer and better able to get things back together. I want him to walk away from a bad episode knowing that he is OK, and that he can handle his frustration rather than it handling him.

◆ ◆ ◆

The following story can be seen as a metaphor for personal resiliency and emotional fortitude:

> One day a mule fell into a dry well. There was no way to lift the mule out, so the farmer directed his boys to bury the mule in the well. But the mule refused to be buried. As the boys would throw dirt on the mule, it would simply trample the dirt. Very soon enough dirt had been thrown into the well that the mule walked out.

That which was intended to bury the mule was the very means by which it rose. This story speaks as much to the experience of parents of ADHD children as it does to that of the children themselves. As parents, we sometimes feel like we are being "buried alive" by all the problems caused by ADHD. It is not that our children intend to smother us; rather, the symptoms emerging from ADHD are themselves suffocating to both the parent and the child.

Like the mule, a surprising number of children with ADHD refuse to be emotionally buried by negative feedback, parental disapproval, isolation, and academic difficulty. Somehow these children walk into their adult lives making significant contributions to their communities and chosen vocations. It is believed that these children often had at least one person who unconditionally believed in them and supported the competent and capable side of their personality. It is amazing what one person, especially a father, can do to ensure a child's success.

Children with disabilities, whether emotional or physical, can often overcome sizable odds if they believe a parent believes in them. Like a chameleon who takes on the color of its environment as a form of protection against danger, children with ADHD often take on the attitudes and beliefs of their parents. Children often define themselves by how they are defined. If they perceive that they are considered "bad," a "waste of time," "worthless," or only tolerated, they will begin living out this belief by seeking out negative experiences. The father of an 11-year-old son describes this phenomena:

Jake is hanging around a pretty unmotivated crowd. You know, black T-shirts, jungle boots, and strange haircuts. He is handsome and smart, but chooses to be around these kids that appear to have little drive in life other than hanging out and getting by. I don't approve of it, but if I push too hard, he'll probably rebel even more. He could have any friend or be in any peer group he wants, but he is the BMOC [Big Man on Campus] with these kids. His friends don't challenge him. He is the witty, tall, cool guy in the group. He is definitely their leader. They all seem to follow him like a faithful puppy. If he was in a different peer group, he may not be idolized like he currently is. I am not sure why he is making these choices about friends.

We have had a pretty strained relationship over the years. It's hard for me to be supportive of a kid who doesn't seem to care about other people's feelings and views. I think Jake is an angry kid. He blows up frequently at his mother and me. For the most part I either ignore him or get angry back. It doesn't seem very productive.

This father seems to be describing a boy who struggles with issues of self-control, respect for self, and respect for others. These issues are rooted in Jake's image of himself and his belief in what type of social and peer group risks are worth taking. A child who receives emotionally nurturing discipline will begin to develop, over time, similar levels of personal discipline as it relates to choosing social and peer groups. For instance, if a child encounters inconsistent or punitive discipline at home, he will be more inclined to tolerate a lack of discipline in his peers. This may in turn serve to strengthen a lack of self-discipline in the child.

This father feels overwhelmed by his son's choices about personal appearance and peer relations. This has led to a mutual exchange of anger and resentment, which reinforces the father's perception of his son's negative choices. In the words of Oliver Wendell Holmes, "The great thing in the world is not so much where we stand, as in what direction we are moving."

If we continue to have unproductive or angry interactions with our sons, the direction we are headed will be a place of ongoing and unrelenting struggle. Remember the old saying, "No matter where you go, there you are."

With all of the above said, it is also important to understand that a small minority of children with ADHD will not thrive emotionally or psychologically even in the face of heroic parental efforts. Whether it is a function of the child's temperament, personality, predisposition, peer influences, or a combination of these, some children do not respond positively. The choices they make, coupled with an apparent lack of personal discipline, keeps these children caught in a cycle of negative feedback, social inappropriateness, academic failure, and even legal problems.

As one father of a 13-year-old boy stated:

I don't know what else we can do. We have tried family therapy, individual therapy, private school, home schooling, etc. It's not like we have been unwilling to help David address his issues and the family issues. His behavior has been disruptive to everyone. I have two other children who frankly are not a problem. I resent all my energy, time, and money going toward David's negative situations. It's almost like rewarding the bad stuff. I've made it clear when he is willing to take responsibility for his part in all this, I am willing to support him. That means working in therapy, with the family, and cutting out the negative crap. Period. That's it. I am washed-out. He knows where I stand, ADHD or not, there is never and will never be an excuse for some of the stuff he does to us, himself, and others.

◆ ◆ ◆

ATTITUDE IS EVERYTHING

There is a saying: "The pessimist looks at opportunities and sees difficulties, the optimist looks at difficulties and sees opportunities." Attitudes can be the catalyst to action. They guide our behavior and our behavior guides our relationships. There is also a saying, "If you believe it, it is true." Our beliefs and attitudes translate into action and behavior. If you believe things will not work out, they probably will not. If you believe that things will have a positive outcome, they usually do, in some form or fashion.

We've got the clowns running the circus. (page 62)

Coaches are fond of saying, "Attitude is everything." When things are not going particularly well, you might hear them say, "Hey, what's the 'tude all about." Attitude drives the quality and intensity of our interaction with others.

Take a moment to think about the attitudes you bring to bear on the relationship you have with your son. For example, do you have the attitude that boys will be boys and your son is really no different than any other child his age—he is just more rambunctious, or louder, or more excitable?

Problems can develop if your attitude is out of sync with either the reality of your child's behavior or with the perceptions of your child's mother, school officials, coaches, or neighbors. If you believe that your son must listen and obey your instructions, yet he is unable to do so, your attitude may be that he is purposely defying your authority. The reality may be that he is not intentionally defiant, but rather in the midst of an emotional surge or too distracted to follow through. As this father describes, attitude shifts can pay important dividends:

I generally do not get hooked by his volatile behavior the way I used to. I realize that due to ADHD, he often cannot help it when his emotions run away with him. I used to be extremely confrontational with him when he didn't listen or didn't follow through with something. Now, when he has a problem, I really try to remember that he can't necessarily help it, and that if he could he would not be acting that way. His attitude and behavior in other situations clearly indicate he wants to do well. It is also clear how much it pains him when his emotions run away with him. The other day he blew up at me at baseball practice when I calmly pointed out a better way to catch the ball. He stormed off expressing a lot of anger toward me. About five minutes later I walked over to him, while he was hunched over playing with a stick in the dirt. I rubbed his back and asked what was going on. He just looked at me with tear filled eyes and said, "I don't know." He really doesn't know, but I know at that moment he realized it was OK.

If your attitude is that your son needs more intense guidance and monitoring during difficult times, and that he is not "acting out" on purpose, the probability is that, with your guidance, he will gain control quicker, internalize more deeply your modeling and instruction, and more frequently display self-directed and self-disciplined behavior. One father noted:

I take things personally with Mike. When he gives me a scowling look, or rejects my help or comments, I get very defensive. I sort of want to sulk, or I want him to run over and say, "Gee, Dad, I am sorry for hurting your feelings, or rejecting your opinion." When I shift my attitude and realize he doesn't mean it personally, I shake it off, and he shakes it off, and we move on. I am usually the one who holds on to the anger or resentment. When I shake or even laugh it off, 10 minutes later he is over snuggling or asking an upbeat question.

This is a wonderful example of how an attitude shift can make the difference for a father and son between feeling isolated and letting go of the negative experience to make way for more rewarding interaction. Letting go also sends the message to your son that he is OK, that he is *having* a bad moment, not that he *is* the bad moment.

Like much in life, effective and rewarding parenting is mostly mental. Success in parenting, defined as raising self-disciplined, compassionate, and motivated children, starts with understanding your child's strengths and having a "can do" attitude. It is important to remember that raising a self-disciplined child often hinges on the level of personal discipline and restraint conveyed by the parent. As one father states:

As the father of a child who has ADHD, I feel we are held to a higher standard than parents whose kids do not have any obvious disability. I don't like to think of my two sons as having a disability, but the fact is they do. Once I got beyond the ADHD diagnosis, and realized there is a whole lot I can do for them that I previously was not doing, I had to change not only my behavior but my thinking. These two beautiful boys have neurological and developmental difficulties. I remember sitting late one night in my chair just fixated on this, and thinking about this over and over. I wanted to scream! I thought, how can I really help these two characters who have such a large satchel to carry through life? This is what I thought.

After doing some reading and certainly talking with my wife, I realized there was a huge amount I could personally do to ensure that my boys could develop to the best of their personal ability. The most difficult thing for me was remembering that they struggled holding it together emotionally, they were impulsive and could not stay focused on anything for very long. This was particularly hard because I am such a believer in remaining emotionally calm and levelheaded.

I remember my father being so rigid, not showing emotion to others. For him, I think, it represented some type of emotional weakness. So I was battling all these early-learning and belief systems as well as my own attitude about how a son should be. I have learned that relying on "shoulds" and having a fixed attitude about what must be can torpedo a relationship with these kids. I got a sense of what they could handle and accomplish, and what was going to be difficult for them. Based on this we devised a daily structure that would play to their developmental strengths.

Creating the environment within which a child with ADHD can thrive and prosper emotionally requires a tremendous amount of patience, endurance, and positive attitude on the part of the parents. Personal discipline in our children emerges from multiple influences, the most important of which is parental modeling and a perception by the child that his parents believe in him. Because it can be so difficult at times raising children with ADHD, parents can easily find themselves wandering down an unfulfilling and stressful path. When you feel your path is strewn with difficulty, remember these words:

> Do not follow where the path may lead. Go, instead, where there is no path and leave the trail.

Chapter 6

MANAGING ADHD: BEHAVIOR MANAGEMENT STRATEGIES

As discussed in the previous chapter, discipline is an integral part of parenting and caring for our children, and consists of two specific forms of interaction with children. In that chapter we focused on the "emotional" response. In this chapter, we will address behavior management strategies. There are hundreds of behavior management programs directed toward improving inappropriate behavior or strengthening desired behaviors.

While they do respond positively to consistent behavior management strategies, children with ADHD present unique challenges, as they don't always respond consistently or as expected by their parents. Fathers of sons with ADHD frequently wrestle with the question of how to establish a system of effective, positive discipline that supports their sons, yet encourages them to assume some of the responsibility for their actions.

As Thomas Phelan states in the introduction to his book, *One-Two-Three Magic*, "Children don't come with a training manual. Adults, therefore, need to know how to handle children's difficult behavior, how to encourage their good behavior, and how to handle the inevitable sidetrack of testing and manipulation. This must be done in a manner that is fair, perfectly clear, and not abusive. This may be a difficult task, but it is critical to peaceful coexistence. It is also critical to developing each child's ability to enjoy life and maintain healthy self-esteem." So how does a father of a child with ADHD accomplish this?

Fathers use different parenting styles depending on their own backgrounds, family experience, education, temperament, and inclination. However, in talking to numerous dads, we found an element of agreement about the most effective way to reduce problematic behaviors. It is the voices of these fathers that you will hear in this chapter. These fathers have grappled with managing ADHD-related behaviors on a daily basis. They are the experts.

These fathers learned that managing ADHD effectively was a process that required **time**—time for the development of personal maturity in both father and son and time for fathers to become educated about the impact of ADHD on their sons. They also learned the importance of the **desire to change** previous negative forms of interaction or discipline and of the belief that these changes will lead to a more positive relationship. But how do you set up a behavior management system that enhances the father–son relationship and is supportive rather than punitive?

Fathers almost unanimously report that one of the most effective and positive behavior management tools they use is **remaining calm** when their son is agitated or having problems. Although this can be difficult to accomplish, it has a way of deescalating the problem quickly, without negative fallout for the child.

I noticed the most important behavior management tool has to do with the way I approach a negative or inappropri-

STRATEGY 1

Remain Calm

◆ Remaining calm is the #1 measure a parent can take.

◆ Become as educated as possible on what ADHD is all about. If you understand how it influences your son's behavior, you will better understand his responses.

◆ If you feel you're reaching a boiling point, TAKE A BREAK, LET YOUR SPOUSE DO IT, OR COME BACK TO IT WHEN YOU ARE CALMER.

ate situation. Before Chris was diagnosed and medicated, I would go ballistic on him if he disobeyed, talked back, or caused problems. I became so aggravated that I just would lose it. This in turn would send him even deeper into a bad attitude or defiance. The louder he got, the louder I got, and so forth.

There was a tremendous amount of stress and tension in the house. Now, since I have learned more about ADHD, and realize my previous way of dealing with Chris was at best ineffective, I now deal with him in a different way. If he starts spiraling out of control, I reduce my negativity and greet his intensity with a calm manner and reason. The change in his behavior in response to this is remarkable. There is very little tension in the house, and if he does something really inappropriate, I will calmly send him to time-out. The whole way of dealing with him now is different and productive, especially when he feels overwhelmed by his emotions.

When Dave is displaying defiance or is acting out, my first instinct is to grab him by the back of the neck, scream in his face, and send him to his room. I used to do this quite regularly with him, as a control measure. Over time I tried to bring a more reasoned approach to the relationship when he is going through an emotional flame-out, and this has helped tremendously.

Children with ADHD have a tendency to respond aggressively to situations they perceive as frustrating. This provides an added reason to remove violent actions such as spanking, hitting, grabbing, or screaming as discipline strategies when dealing with your child's inappropriate behavior. By meeting a child's out-of-control behavior with similar out-of-control behavior, a father models and reinforces aggressive responses. By modeling control and appropriate anger management, the father provides the child the opportunity to learn how to control impulses and emotions. By taking the emotional lead, the father can diffuse potentially difficult situations.

The adult has to take the lead in establishing control in the family and in the child's life. There are always going to be bumps along the way, and the child has to feel secure that when he can't control himself, you will be there as an anchor to help steady the listing ship. When I am with Jace, I'll say, "Look, you have to have this done by tomorrow and if you don't want me in the room, I'll leave. If you do want me here, I'll be happy to help in any way I can." I don't pressure him to conform when he can't control himself.

A WORD ABOUT SPANKING

Spanking is a controversial subject in the field of parenting. Some professionals advocate it, while others consider it harmful. When parents decide to use spanking as a disciplining tool, they make the choice to model aggressive behavior as a control strategy. Forcefully imposing your will upon a person thus becomes acceptable and condones a certain level of violent behavior. The use of spanking as a tool is not a neutral or passive response to dealing with your son's ADHD-related behavior.

When spanking is employed out of anger, as a first line of defense, it becomes an adult "temper tantrum" and teaches our children that when we are angry, we hit other people. There is also an emotional downside to spanking, especially when the only child in the family being spanked is the one with ADHD. This may reinforce the feelings of shame that often accompany ADHD.

Along with being calm, fathers also mentioned that **preparing for transitions** or new events often keeps their sons from having problems. When prepared ahead of time, the child knows what to expect and has the opportunity to comment on the situation, practice responses, or go over the "rules" of appropriate behavior. If this discussion is accompanied by consistency and clarity, the likelihood of having problems is significantly reduced. An excellent example of how this works can be seen in the following father's comments:

I don't get excited when Jon slips up or is having an off moment. I used to jump on him any and every time he did something that didn't meet my expectations. I realize now that he is doing his best and should be applauded for that. We always discuss what we are going to do before we do it—what kind of things might be discouraging or problematic. He prepares himself for the event, whether it's going to the movies or a baseball game. He knows what to expect. Before, we would go to the movies and he would want all this stuff or to play just one more video game and I would get angry and this cloud of tension would descend on us for the rest of the day. Now we talk about what the limits are. It is amazing the difference it has made in reducing problems. Being clear and consistent has been the best behavior management tool in our relationship.

STRATEGY 2

Prepare Your Child for Transitions

◆ Be aware of potential transitions, for example, as medication is wearing off, going to a mall, leaving for church services, etc.

◆ Discuss the rules, what will happen during the event, what the child can expect, and what the acceptable behavior will be.

◆ DO NOT ASSUME ANYTHING!

◆ Be clear and realistic about consequences if rules are not followed. The consequence should allow your son the opportunity to correct his behavior. For example, going to the car for the remaining three hours of the picnic is not a helpful or instructional consequence; not getting ice cream or a toy he wants is a fair consequence.

Focusing on what the child does well and creating opportunities for success relating to that ability allow the child with ADHD to feel competent, less frustrated, and more successful. This approach can minimize behavioral problems, boost self-esteem, and prevent unfortunate comparisons between siblings. Children should always be accepted for who they are or what they can do rather than rejected for what they are not. Recognizing his child's strengths appears to be an excellent manage-

STRATEGY 3

Focus on What Your Child Does Well

◆ Notice when your son does something right. When children with ADHD do something wrong it is louder, longer, more intense, and more frequent then their non-ADHD peers. The noise and pace of children with ADHD can distract us from noticing the appropriate or "bright" things they are doing.

◆ Whenever possible allow your son to volunteer to help you with projects. When he says, "Hey dad, can I help you cut down the tree, or mulch the lawn, or fix the car, etc., capitalize on his desire to participate and help.

◆ When you notice your son doing something helpful or appropriate, look him in the eyes and point out how terrific it was. You don't have to make a big deal out of it—you merely need to let him know that you know what he is doing. You can also bring this up later as an opportunity for your son to build on that behavior: "Jim, remember yesterday when you took the time to play with little Johnny next door? How would you like to take your little brother upstairs for a bath?

ment tool already realized and used effectively by the father below:

Each of our children is different, and they have to be approached differently. Our daughter is in the gifted program and already in high school is taking college-level courses. She is a self-starter and excels academically. Consequently, we operate at a totally different level with her than with our son. There is more of an intellectual exchange, and she is able to grasp complex concepts. Tim, on the other hand, necessitates focusing on smaller bits of information or breaking tasks down into smaller bits. Developmentally, he is not able right now to experience the type of academic success that our daughter does.

He has other strengths, and we focus on those considerably in order for him to experience achievement and a sense of mastery over areas of his life. He is a wonderful athlete, so we focus on making sure he gets a lot of satisfaction from his sports activities and is given all the opportunities to fulfill himself in those pursuits. Academically, we support him in plugging away and doing his best. There is never any comparison between him and his sister.

It is also fortunate that they differ in age quite a bit. So he can feel, and we can create, more distance between her academic ability and Tim's academic struggles. Also, I have learned the defense against volatile behavior is to relax and let him know I am available if he wants me.

Knowing what motivates a child to action is another effective behavior management tool. **Providing choices** seems to help a child "buy in" to desired behaviors.

I give the children, especially Tyler, choices in terms of expected behavior. If we want something done, or not done, the kids will have several choices to pick from. For instance, this morning, I was feeling rushed to get out of the house and Tyler had his socks on and nothing else. I said, "Tyler, you have a choice, be ready to go when the big hand is on 2, or spend a half hour in your room when we get home." Then I asked him to repeat what I had said to make sure he heard me. This strategy tends to be very effective. If I order him to do something, it, more often than not, winds up in some sort of tug-of-war.

STRATEGY 4

Know What Motivates Your Child

◆ Not all children with ADHD respond to positive reinforcement. Your belief that your son *should* respond positively to something doesn't mean that he *will.* Knowing what he likes will help you motivate him. For example, "Hey, Johnny, what would you like to do after dinner?" "I really want to play hide-and-go-seek, Dad." "OK, if you get all your homework done neatly, and help set the table, we will play 20 minutes of hide-and-go-seek."

◆ Negotiate for more thoughtful/reflective behavior. Giving your son the opportunity to choose between things he doesn't want will not increase his motivation. "Mark, what would you really like to do with me and your brother this weekend?" "I would like to go to the batting cages." "OK, are you willing to begin your homework the rest of this week after school without complaining?" "Yes, I will do that." "OK, let's put together a chart that you can mark off each day to indicate you fulfilled your part of the deal."

◆ Motivating your son to act in a particular way is not bribery. Tapping into what he likes to do can naturally reinforce what you like him to do.

By **asking the child what he has heard,** this father was able to be sure that they both were clear on expectations. However, this type of strategy can have its pitfalls. For one thing, the father will need to be consistent in following through on the half hour of time-out when they get home, if that is what the son

STRATEGY 5

Provide Choices

◆ Choices allow your son to feel a sense of personal control over his behavior. For example, "Paul, I would like you to choose what chore you want to do today: cut the lawn, trim the hedges, or empty all the trash in the house." This gives him a chance to choose what he feels most motivated to do. You can also put all the chores in a basket, and he can choose one or two randomly. This allows him to feel that he is choosing rather than being told what he *must* do.

◆ The language we use in giving choices makes a difference. For example, "Cut the lawn, wash the car, or go to your room" is not seen as an incentive to act appropriately. Giving real choices does not mean the child has the option *not* to do the chore. He must choose and complete one or the other.

chose. In addition, this type of situation can set one up for more frustration and failure in light of the busy schedules we all keep. Always being consistent can be difficult in a demanding life where time is a luxury.

As we have mentioned over and over again, following through and **being consistent** are the stanchions necessary to reinforce desired behaviors. Like all of us at certain times, some fathers find this particularly difficult.

I remember a scene about which I felt the worst, where I was, really just was, totally frustrated. The specifics of what brought it about I don't even recall. It was just another one of the interminable situations. Ultimately I had reached the end of my rope in relying on these coached behavioral strategies. They talked about diffusing conflict and taking the high ground as an adult, etc. I basically took Jeff aside and threatened him. I said, "Look, we have tried everything with you. Nothing has worked. You do it again and I promise I will beat you." Even this had little effect on him. I didn't follow through and beat him. I just ignored and distanced myself from him. It feels like I am being brought to my emotional knees.

◆ ◆ ◆

This father found the behavioral strategies he tried in managing his son's ADHD behaviors to be ineffective. It seems from the description above that this father believes that nothing is going to make a difference. Threatening bodily harm, the last strategy used by this father, also failed. As noted, ADHD can bring a father to his "emotional knees." It is important to recognize that one cannot bully a son into a behavior or a change in attitude. Once a father realizes this, and becomes more accepting of his son's limitations, he can place himself in a position of support.

The following two families demonstrate that if parents are consistent, traditional behavior management strategies are very effective. Consistency in employing the management strategy can determine the difference between success and failure.

We have never been spankers. Beyond the typical swat on the butt when there was a dangerous situation like running in the road, we rarely put a hand on our children. We relied on the recommended and prescribed behavior modification techniques that we picked up through counseling and support groups. You know time-out, charts, tokens, and all kinds of rewards. It really does work. Mark is much more aware of his behavior, and tries to control it in order to receive the rewards that he wants. Right now he tries to control his behavior for external rewards. I think as he gets older it will become self-reinforcing and an everyday part of his life.

The most important thing we do in our home regarding behavior management is treat the children equally. If they are doing something well, they get a lot of praise. If they are pushing the limits, they get sanctions. We remove them from the environment or deprive them of things that they like to do. Just because Eddie has ADHD, and the other kids do not, is not a reason to single him out or treat him differently. He does require more of my time than the other kids, but that often occurs in a very positive way. I give him the opportunity to reconnect with me and the family if he is having a tough time. He responds well to this, and really tries to control himself, or he will remove himself if he sees that he is having a control problem. I think that is the most remarkable thing of all. For an eight-year-old to leave the room or go outside because he is having a hard time holding it together is a pretty remarkable thing.

Indeed, this does sound remarkable, but as we have seen over and over again, effectiveness depends more on the consistent use of management strategies than on the type of strategy used. As noted below, there is an important relationship between the degree to which a father is consistent and the level of difficulty experienced by his son. The greater the consistency in the relationship, the less overall problems the child seems to experience.

Something that has been helpful in terms of my relationship with Ben is being consistent in what I do and say. I don't completely understand the neurological difficulties he is experiencing, but actually I don't need to, fully. I know that he needs me to be consistent. It's made a huge difference just breaking the simple, commonsense things down and sticking with it and trying to be consistent, so that the kids know the structures that they have to work within. Limiting

surprises and discussing things ahead of time, before we do
things, really reduces problems.

STRATEGY 6

Be Consistent

◆ Consistency is the basis of maintaining a healthy,
  enjoyable, and positive relationship with your son.
  If you can consistently remain calm, follow though
  on what you say, and model problem-solving strategies, there is a high probability that you will have
  a satisfying relationship. If one day you are calm
  and the next day you explode and then the next
  day you totally withdraw, your child will not really
  know where he stands in his relationship with you.
  BE CONSISTENT, FAIR, AND CALM, AND YOU
  WILL SEE BIG GAINS.

Another effective tool is **rewarding positive behaviors.** This
allows your child to internalize a sense of control. Over time,
he will find the positive behaviors to be personally rewarding
and will demonstrate those behaviors more often. Focusing on
the positive allows your child to anticipate rewards for appropriate behavior instead of expecting punishment for negative
behavior.

Rewarding positive behavior does not necessarily mean that
your son will repeat the behavior. Remember, children with
ADHD tend to be impulsive, hyperactive, and inattentive. Positive reinforcement enhances their feelings of self-esteem. It is
not an absolute predictor that behavior will be repeated in the
future.

STRATEGY 7

Reward Positive Behaviors

◆ There are countless ways to reward the type of behavior you feel is appropriate. For example, "OK, Stevie, if you read for 15 minutes each day between now and Friday, you can choose from one of these three things to do on Saturday, or come up with some of your own ideas."

◆ The more you reward positive behaviors, the more personally rewarding your relationship with your son will be.

◆ Once you say you will reward something positive your son has done, do not take away the reward if he displays negative behavior after the fact. Always follow through on rewarding positive behavior. You may have to postpone giving the reward until the negative episode passes, but it is critical to reinforce that the reward is going to be given. Your son will then have an incentive to move past the negative attitude or behavior quickly.

Although rough moments will occur, a focus on what the child is doing "right" can become the defining factor in the father–son relationship. As one father notes, negative or problematic behaviors happen much less frequently when the father is attending to what the child is doing well:

I tend to naturally concentrate on rewards versus punishment. I have found that Jeff really responds to rewards. I go out of my way to celebrate something positive he has done. If he is caught in a bad space, I will use time-out or remove him from TV or video games, but I find that happens very infrequently. I pay attention to when he is doing things the right way. It is amazing what you can catch your children doing right versus what they do wrong. This has been particularly helpful because Jeff has a tendency to get under people's skin. Celebrating the good stuff has been very helpful.

◆ ◆ ◆

A father's **support** during difficult emotional times conveys the message to the child that he is OK. The father's willingness to remain "in the trenches" during the stressful moments seems to pay off large dividends. In addition, the use of creative strategies to help loosen up the moment can encourage the child to move beyond that moment more quickly and with more positive emotional results.

◆ ◆ ◆

One of the best management tools for me is just sticking with Josh when he is doing something. Even if it is painful and he isn't "getting it," or following directions, or whatever, he needs to know that I am there and trying to help. I simply let him know that I am there if he needs me. Previously, I would try to browbeat him into conformity. Now, I just stay with him and try to help him focus. I use a timer if we are doing homework, and when it goes off he can get up and run around and do push-ups, or step outside for a couple of minutes. This breaks the task up and is respectful of his needs. After the break we are back at it again. Many times he will keep working after the buzzer goes off. I think just knowing he has permission to stretch, eases his mind and lets him focus. Every kid has to feel he can conquer what he is doing, or at least master it to some degree. If not, then he is not going to give it his all.

◆ ◆ ◆

We are getting better at dealing with some of Todd's behaviors. Before we would crash into each other like rams. Now,

STRATEGY 8

Be Supportive

◆ When possible and appropriate, acknowledge that you realize your son is having a tough time or struggling to hold it together. "I know this is really hard for you right now. When you are ready, let's work together to figure out a solution." Or, "I know this is very difficult on you right now, and I am also angry, so when we both cool off let's work something out together." Or, "Before you start yelling at me about what I just said, try asking a question to find out what I meant. It seems you are reacting without getting all the information." This allows your son to feel supported even though there is a high level of intensity and emotion.

◆ When your son is supported, the message conveyed is that even though he is having a difficult moment, it will pass. He doesn't feel trapped by his negative attitude and behavior.

◆ Another form of support is allowing your own anger to pass as quickly as possible. If you hold onto your anger, your son will continue to feel ashamed. Moving past your anger will allow your son to move past his.

◆ If you are finding it difficult to take a neutral stance, seek the support of your spouse, a counselor, reading material, or a friend. It is difficult to always be supportive, especially during intense emotional experiences. Having your own reliable support systems can be very helpful.

we say, "OK, Todd, this is unacceptable behavior. This is not the way to act toward your family, your friends, or in public. What you are feeling, we need to talk about, and when you are ready, let's talk. But right now you need to go for a walk or go to your room to cool off and collect yourself." At some point, we realized that confronting him and going toe-to-toe had negative returns. The new approach is an attempt to calm the waters, clear the air, and allow for discussion. So far, he seems to rally around this approach. He has even said that he feels more understood by his mother and me.

◆ ◆ ◆

Setting up a system that works, that demonstrates a caring attitude, and that leaves all parties with their dignity intact is worth striving for.

◆ ◆ ◆

I think as my son has gotten older, we have both matured. I don't force my opinion on him anymore or force the situation. I spend a few more minutes analyzing what is going on. This gives us both time to gather our thoughts and calm down. It definitely avoids escalation. I find there are very few situations that we cannot resolve calmly and satisfactorily. I think one of the most important aspects of my relationship with Tony is my consistency. I really try to address issues with him from a more supportive and neutral position. I listen and I am honest with him about how I feel, but I don't dump my disappointment all over him. I think I provide a much safer and supportive place for him now.

◆ ◆ ◆

THE GREATEST GIFT

Keeping all these tools in mind when dealing with a son who is experiencing anger and frustration as a result of his ADHD is extremely difficult. It is important to acknowledge this difficulty, but also to understand that our sons are depending on us.

Respecting our sons for who they are is the beginning of a better and more significant relationship with them. In the words of one father, it is the greatest gift we have to offer:

I know how frustrating it has been raising Ed. I would think most fathers of ADHD children would struggle in the area of maintaining the necessary degree of patience. I also think fathers have great expectations for their sons. If there is a chink in the armor or there is some part that somebody has said is rusty or damaged, then the father sees the son in a different, more deficient light. I think that many fathers at that point will begin applying more pressure for the child to conform and "be normal." It is fitting square pegs into round holes. Once this dynamic begins, the father and son are going to feel more or less whipped. Although it can be the hardest thing for a father to do, accepting and respecting the abilities of his child is the greatest gift he can offer.

SUMMARY OF
BEHAVIOR MANAGEMENT STRATEGIES

- ◆ Remain calm
- ◆ Prepare your child for transitions
- ◆ Focus on what your child does well
- ◆ Know what motivates your child
- ◆ Provide choices
- ◆ Be consistent
- ◆ Reward positive behaviors
- ◆ Be supportive

Chapter 7

MANAGING ADHD: MEDICATION ISSUES

I HAVE GOTTEN MY SON BACK

The following story is typical of the diagnosis and treatment of ADHD in an eight-year-old boy. It also presents his father's reaction to the process.

We started having Peter tested in second grade, as a result of some developmental problems, if not real learning disabilities, that showed up his first real academic year in first grade. He was diagnosed as having ADHD in second grade and started on Ritalin [one of the stimulants used to treat ADHD] shortly after he was diagnosed. I was somewhat skeptical at first about putting him on medication, especially since Peter was so young. My wife felt if there was a pill that could make things better for him, then put him on it.

I do not subscribe to the belief of "better living through chemistry" but I went along with putting him on medication. I felt as long as there was no serious downside, we might as well give it a try. Since this is not a condition that you can detect through a blood test or MRI, the only way to monitor the course of ADHD is by the child's behavior and Peter had plenty of trouble with that. Once he began taking the medication he did seem more compliant and better able to attend to tasks. Previously, he was forever forgetting or losing or misplacing things and, in order to get his work done, required a lot of additional support.

The medication has slowed him down so he reflects more on what he needs to do. His ability to organize his responsibilities has come a long way. I credit the education, behavior management tools, and tutoring for the difference in his grades and behavior. Without medication, I don't think he could have slowed down enough to take advantage of the tutoring or follow some of the behavioral management tasks. He is doing well, and I notice a difference in his attitude and behavior when he is not on medication. He just seems better adjusted and happier all the way around, and I feel that I have gotten back my son.

When fathers talk about their feelings about their sons and ADHD, it is evident that they were aware of a developmental difference in their sons prior to the diagnosis and saw definitive changes after the onset of treatment. Their sons did not seem to fit in with others around them. That "gut" feeling that something was wrong is what caused many fathers to seek help or evaluations for their sons. They were aware of differences and concerned enough about their sons to seek treatment. But let them tell it in their own words:

With medication, John's metabolism has slowed down enough for him to both conform to the larger societal demands as well as live up to his developmental potential. Before taking medication he was a five-year-old in an eight-year-old's body. He especially seemed to be delayed emotionally, in comparison to his same age peers. He is maturing as well as being on medication, so he is learning how to handle his world in a much more constructive and positive manner. He is learning to problem solve effectively and deal with frustration and delayed gratification much more reasonably. In many ways, he even seems more mature than the kids he hangs around. The ADHD has really forced us early on to be aware of John's personal development, and not take anything for granted. I think in many ways, John has behaviorally benefited from us being so aware of what was and was not developmentally appropriate for him at certain stages.

◆　◆　◆

I think in the beginning I resisted placing Tim on medication because I did not want to admit that my son had a disability and that he was going to be different, by virtue of taking the medication, from the other kids in his class. I wanted to believe that he could find some way to compensate for the attentional and behavioral problems, or that we could find out some way. I remember we put him into therapy hoping that he would "decide" to concentrate more. What therapy

I sometimes think of myself as his
"emotional air bag." (page 83)

did was indicate even further that Tim would be limping through life for quite a while unless he got the necessary support that he needed now by taking medication. I just wanted to believe that this was some kind of developmental blip on the screen that would go away if we all tried really hard. Well, we are all trying really hard, and even with medication Tim has his work cut out for him. It is evident, however, that he has been able to achieve and even surpass a lot of what his peers are doing. So I feel extremely grateful for his progress and stability.

I think that the principal thing that you must accept or remember is that whatever you choose to label the problem, dealing with a person with ADHD is like dealing with someone who has a broken leg. He is experiencing a handicap in a part of his body that needs special attention. These kids are the same way. There are things that they cannot do. Their body or brain is not going to allow it unless they are on medicine and/or until they grow older and can learn to cope with the environment. I believe, most of all, the parent really makes the difference in how the child feels about himself in relation to the larger world. I know with Joey that he feels genuinely loved and cared for regardless of what and who he is. I have learned that I cannot and should not try to push him beyond what he is capable of. We encourage him to move at his own speed and do what he can. The kids let us know what they are ready for and how capable they can be at achieving the task.

These fathers are aware that the use of medication has allowed their child to achieve and excel in ways that were previously blocked.

I think it is important to understand why we put our son on medication. We put him on medication because we want him to focus and gain a certain level of personal maturity. It is hoped that, at some point, once he receives the benefits of the drug, he can stop taking medication. Hopefully, the medication will allow him to gain the necessary skills he will need to succeed in an increasingly competitive and difficult world. Medication can slow him down enough for him to get a lot of positive feedback and learn some valuable ways of treating and interacting with other people. He genuinely wants to please others and positively participate with other kids. He is a great athlete, and the medication has slowed him down enough to concentrate and take in information regarding the fundamental skills he needs to excel athleti- cally. Although I don't like my son to have to take medica- tion, I am always aware of what he was like before he was on medication, as well as the transformative effect the medication has had on both his and my life.

Table 14 lists some of the things medication can do for your son. Despite knowing this, the decision to use medication re- mains one of the most difficult decisions facing you as the fa- ther of a child with ADHD. Even though the effects of the medication are positive, many fathers continue to question their decision or worry about the long-term impact of the medication.

I would have to consider one of the toughest decisions of my adult life was deciding to place our son on medication. I initially had a very strong emotional resistance to the whole concept of medication—especially medicating a four-year- old. However, on an objective, more rational level I realized this isn't forever or doesn't have to be forever. We ought to give it a try and see how it works. If it does what it is sup- posed to do, then we would be remiss not to offer it to Paul. For us, it was an obviously positive decision and outcome. Paul's confidence level and overall attitude eclipses his former self. It's made a huge difference in all of our lives.

As they recount in several of these stories, some fathers were very reluctant to use medication, even though they knew that

TABLE 14

Medication Can . . .

◆ Slow down hyperactive functioning so your child can relax and complete age appropriate tasks, such as, build with blocks, complete homework, etc.

◆ Reduce impulsivity so that your child can "look before he leaps."

◆ Increase attention span so your child will want to engage in tasks previously experienced as frustrating, such as waiting for a turn, participating in class, interacting socially with peers, and following through on expectations.

◆ Much like glasses do for nearsightedness, allow your child to focus and attend to pertinent social and academic information.

their sons suffered from a neurological problem that could be stabilized by the medication. Fathers did not want to believe that their sons required the ongoing use of medication to help them gain and maintain control. Even when the fathers permitted the use of medication, and saw marked improvement in their sons' behavior and ability, they were still reluctant to use it consistently. This ambivalence confirms the great emotional difficulty involved in deciding to place a child on medication. These fathers, however, soon realized the greater benefit to their sons and put their own hesitations behind them:

Stevie was diagnosed three years ago and was immediately put on stimulant medication. At first, we used it only occasionally because we wanted to see what the overall effects of medication would be, and if he could function without being on it all the time. So we initially didn't give it on weekends or when he was home from school. It was recommended that he remain on it twice a day on weekends. We began to notice that he really did have all-around better days when he was on medication, and his temperament was a lot more even and agreeable. He could focus on his required tasks and complete them with relative ease, and it slowed him down enough to feel a sense of control over his world. I just felt uncomfortable keeping him on it so, despite the positive results, I was loath to give it to him regularly. As I think back, I probably wasn't doing him any favors—I mean by putting my needs or worries above his general well-being, principally because the medication had a positive effect. It wasn't like he had a bad reaction to it, and the professionals said keep giving it to him anyway.

The only thing that I was slow on or had some denial about was seeking out medical help for Jacob. I didn't like the thought of my son being on medication. I had done some reading about hyperactive children, and the majority of the literature said your child was going to be medicated if, in fact, he was hyperactive. I wanted to try other things before bringing him to the doctor. I don't like chemicals, and I don't like medication that is modified by chemicals. I suppose that happens to be a shortcoming of mine. I also think it delayed getting the type of help that Jacob needed. Even though we now have Jacob on medication, I think you need to get them off as quickly as possible and let them adjust to the world they are going to live in without relying on popping pills every time they are upset or have bad feelings. Otherwise, as they get older, they may rely solely on using a pill to cope with life's problems. It just bothers me that he is going to have to take this pill to perform in life.

I was also worried about using Ritalin because no medication is a guarantee, and they really haven't resolved the side effects associated with the medicine. I felt it was depriving him of his appetite. When he isn't on the medicine, his appetite is excellent. To be honest we haven't been giving it to him as regularly as we should, so it is hard to develop a stable routine that lets him eat either before or after the medication or after it wears off. The other piece is that he needs medication for focusing not for direct behavioral problems. It's not like he is standing on the desk in class. If we forgot to give him an afternoon dose of Ritalin I could not tell the difference in his behavior, although I may not be the most objective source.

Conversely, putting their child on medication generated in some fathers a sense of relief. They reported that the use of medication allowed them the opportunity to develop, or at least to approximate, the type of relationship with their son that they had always wanted. These fathers describe how they began to be supportive and available in new ways to their sons. The fathers also had a definite positive response to their sons' attitude and behavior changes.

Before Kevin was diagnosed, things were pretty rough in terms of his behavior and ability to follow basic rules and structure. After the diagnosis, I remember feeling this real sense of relief — that, number one, he is not a bad or purposely defiant kid; and, two, there was a medication with a proven track record that could help him get some control and reduce his problem behaviors. Once we started him on medication, it was as if he was a different kid. He was attentive, respectful, cuddly, inquisitive, and fun. The air of tension that hung over our house lifted. I also noticed that I felt different about him. I looked forward to seeing him when I got home from work, or I wanted to be around him more. He still has his moments, but they are short in duration and nothing compared to before.

Although medication increases functioning in certain areas, it is not a panacea for the multiple issues that a child with ADHD must confront. As some fathers found, the mere fact that a child is on medication does not mean that he will automatically conform to social and academic demands. Stimulant medication gives the child "a boost up"; it is not a magical substance that transforms the child into someone perfect.

When Jimmy started on medication, I had this fantasy that it would somehow "fix" all problems he was having. Certainly the medication has had a positive effect on him, but it gives him the strength to hang on tighter and pull himself up, rather than boost him to the top. These medications have not evened him out in the traditional sense, he is still pretty intense, and can dip into some old behavior. What is troubling is that once his teachers learn that he is on medication it is like, "OK, now we can expect him to be a little angel and not disturb us while we attend to all the other kids in the class." Fortunately, the medication allows his personality and energy to remain intact, so he slows down, and is more thoughtful, but he still is a boy with funny ideas and a sense of adventure. The teachers just don't seem to fully understand what ADHD is, and that supporting Jimmy is an ongoing issue. It doesn't stop once he swallows a pill.

My son is a big kid for his age, so other kids in his class could be intimidated by him. The teachers were complaining that he was aggressive on the playground and the other kids were scared of him. Plus, he was disruptive in class, to the point where he either was sitting in his desk in the corner of the class or working in the principal's office. After we had him evaluated, the doctor said that Ritalin would slow him down and allow him to experience a sense of control and success in school. In the beginning, I just thought he was being a boy. I didn't see all the need for alarm and concern. I am very physical and wrestle with him a lot, so I thought that maybe I was the instigator in his behavior. As it turns out, his behavior was different from the other kids in the class, and it seemed he really couldn't hold it together. Since he has been on medication, the reports from school are much more positive, although he still has a tendency to be aggressive on the playground. We are using behavior management techniques to help control some of this. I can honestly say that the medication has given him a sense of control. You can see it in the way he carries himself, in the things he says, and in his basic attitude.

Behavior management strategies, as we discussed in Chapter 6, are certainly useful tools for improving behaviors and helping our sons gain control. Although these strategies are necessary for the child to learn more appropriate behaviors, alone they are not sufficient for many children to gain control and mastery of their environment. For the majority of children with ADHD, medication has been extremely effective when combined with other tools. The medication allows the child to slow down enough to respond to behavior management strategies or attend to individual or group counseling. Medication enhances the child's probability of success in the most important areas of his life—sports, school, family, and peer relations.

After our son was diagnosed, we were informed that medication would enhance his performance, attention, and overall general ability level. Before we started the medication, however, and because I was opposed to having him rely on some chemical to socially or academically fit in, we tried a series of behavior management tactics to help him establish control over the areas he was having so much trouble in. We asked his teacher to put him in the front of the class to reduce distraction; we had him on a reward system both at school and at home; we asked that he be allowed to run errands for the teacher and clap out erasers, etc. All of these things allowed David to take a significant step forward, but I think when we finally decided to introduce Ritalin, it allowed him to take maybe another two steps forward. We decided on medication because all we were doing just didn't seem to be enough to create the gains we had hoped for David. Since he has been on stimulant medication, there is a noticeable difference in his mood, self-confidence, and willingness to participate in activities he used to shy away from, like organized sports.

◆ ◆ ◆

Frequently fathers find their decision to use medication validated by the behavior and attitude changes they see in their sons. In the following excerpt, a father describes how medication allowed his son to slow down and internalize positive coping strategies:

◆ ◆ ◆

Once Bart was diagnosed, the physician stated that medication would probably provide Bart with the added social and academic boost he needed to feel successful. At first I was reluctant to put him on medication. While my wife took him to another doctor for a second opinion, I went to the library and read several articles on Ritalin and stimulant medication. The evidence seemed to indicate—although there were some articles that were more equivocal—that Ritalin really could make a difference in his functioning on a broad-based level. Based on what we have seen over the past couple of years, the Ritalin clearly has given Bart the chance to feel competent, in control, and pretty successful. In fact, when he is not on the medication, there is a distinct difference in his attitude, emotional state, and level of compliance. As he is getting older, I can see how the medication is allowing him to internalize some ways to cope when he is not on medication.

◆ ◆ ◆

As fathers frequently recognize, it is the combination of medication and personal maturity that helps the child to create and maintain an array of positive coping skills. However, while fathers acknowledge that the medication is effective in modifying certain behaviors, some express concern about their son's reliance on medication to function both socially and academically.

Knowing that my son has to take medication to get along in this world bothers me a lot. I know he needs it by the positive effect it has on his daily functioning, but I still am bothered by his need to use this external substance to function. I am reminded of the movie "Awakening," where the main character could only achieve a normal existence through the use of medication. Eventually the medication stopped having the positive effect of reversing these severe neurological effects, and he returned to his disabled state. I worry that this medication creates an illusion—that what I am seeing really isn't my son, and that eventually the medication will stop working and we will have to adjust to his true nature. There is also a piece that, since I now know how effective the medication can be, I don't want to see him off of it. This obviously creates some confusion for me based on what I just said.

I suppose the most difficult issue for me concerning Jeff's use of medication is that it creates behavior and compliance which are artifacts. By that I mean it isn't really *his* disposition or behavior. So when the medication wears off, we have to adjust our psyche to deal with this kid who is kind of bonkers—behaviorally, that is. It is like he has this emotional meltdown when he is off meds. He becomes loud, acts five years younger than his age. I don't understand some of his questions or thought processes. I mean it's like he really regresses. There is a piece of me that is extremely resentful that Jeffrey and the family have to go through this emotional roller coaster. It just doesn't seem fair. So part of me wants to keep him off medication and learn to deal with him as he is, not as I want him to be or the way the medication makes him temporarily fit in. Granted, the medicine makes a big difference in his personality and willingness to participate appropriately, but I can't help wonder how it must make him feel to know that the only reason he is getting along so well with others and in school is because of the pill he swallows three times a day. He must wonder about his own abilities or inabilities, as it were, to control himself without outside intervention.

It can be difficult for fathers to reconcile the duality they see in their sons' personality on and off stimulants. Is their son the competent, in-control student or the "screw up" who loses things or ruins everything for himself and others?

ADHD is a neurobiological disorder caused by a biochemical abnormality in the brain. Should we relegate our child to being defined by his disorder or alleviate the symptoms and allow him to stand to face life and its challenges? While attention deficits may be seen as normal variants on a continuum, they are proven risk factors for later development of delinquency, depression, drug abuse, and general dissatisfaction with one's accomplishments. Medication significantly reduces these negative consequences.

However, once a child is on medication, people's expectations for conformity can place enormous and often unrealistic pressure on him.

This is ridiculous, he is on medication, but he is still sullen and angry. It's obvious his attitude and behavior have nothing to do with the ADHD, he is just a problem kid.

Placing a child on medication promotes greater attention and less impulsivity; it does not wipe out established feelings born from years of negative experiences and interactions. It also does not replace other management tools; rather, it enhances their effectiveness. On medication the child is better able to learn new behaviors. He still needs an understanding and adaptable environment that meets his unique needs. Too often parents and teachers rely on medication to solve all of the difficulties. This is especially problematic when the medication is not effective.

The medication hasn't been terribly effective. I told his teacher when she asked whether he was going to be on medication this year, "Look, I want you to know that, granted, he has been on medication before. They haven't been particularly successful. They have helped him with some things, but they have had some side effects that we did not think were good. He's been on them and off them over the past couple of years. We are investigating other alternatives and possibly other medications. You have to understand that this isn't something that is real exact. Until we figure this out, we need to know what you can do for him or how we can help you in terms of his class behavior." Some teachers think that medication is the panacea for every kid's problem. Part of what I feel I am doing with the teachers is educating them that even if the kids are on medication, they still are going to require more support and follow-up than most of the other kids.

Many fathers' decision to place their sons on medication is conditional in the beginning. Some fathers report initially not dispensing the medication as prescribed by their physician. They use the medication situationally, rather than develop a consistent schedule. Also many want to get their child off medication as soon as possible. While this is understandable, it may not always be in the best interest of the child.

Generally we don't give our son medication on the weekends. He gets it during the week. From what I gather, the medication is working during the week, in that he is concentrating better in school. At night when he is at home, and off medication, he does not seem to be able to concentrate as well on his homework. In fact, focusing is a major problem for him at night. Even though he is not very focused, my wife pushes him to complete his assignments. He is doing well in school. He is getting B's and A's, and I think that is a marvelous, marvelous improvement. He wants to excel. He is overly, overly concerned about grades. Teachers all tell me that he is preoccupied with grades.

I can't say for sure if the medication makes an appreciable difference in his behavior or not. I am not around him much when he is up in the morning before school and when he gets home. By the time I get home, the medication has worn off. Since we don't give it to him on the weekends, I have to honestly say I don't see a noticeable change. We don't give it to him on the weekends, because he is getting old enough to control a lot of the irritating behavior we used to see when he was younger. Although he seems to always have this edge about him on the weekends, the negative behavior we used to deal with has abated considerably. I suppose the medication could help with the irritability, but I just never really thought about it. We used to give him the medication all the time because he had a lot of inappropriate behaviors cropping up on a consistent basis.

However, to their credit, when faced with the decision, fathers generally put the needs of their sons for medication above their own ambivalence.

I personally have noticed zero difference in his behavior or attitude, although the school reports him being more focused and my wife says that in the morning time and evening time after school he is calmer and compliant. I suppose since I do not see him medicated much, I am not the best objective source. I personally don't think that his unmedicated behavior is bad. I mean he is pretty aggressive and a hard charger. I think those are important qualities to have today, especially in the business climate and world that we live in. I don't particularly mind if he gets loud or opinionated. Since I was never allowed to express myself when I was younger, I wanted to give him the opportunities to cut loose in the ways I couldn't. I also realize that "in order to get along you must go along." And I can say that at times he can be extremely stubborn. The difficulty in focusing and staying on task is the greatest concern for me. If he can't focus and is all over the place, people are going to think that he is dumb or lazy. I want him to avoid a label like that. So if the medicine helps him avoid that label then it is probably worth it.

◆ ◆ ◆

Chapter 8

LIVING WITH ADHD: SURVIVING ADOLESCENCE

For most children and their families, the period of adolescence naturally seems to be filled with turmoil and uncertainty. Although studies indicate that 15–50% of children with ADHD ultimately outgrow their problems, or are at least no longer bothered by the symptoms, most continue to have problems into young adulthood. The changes and stresses inherent in adolescence frequently have an even greater adverse effect on those with ADHD. Mobilizing attention, mastering the necessary organizational skills, and reining in an impulsive behavioral style can seem daunting tasks for the adolescent with ADHD.

While we all wish our children to mature and lead productive lives as independent adults, we worry about how they will accomplish this goal. Adolescents with ADHD tend to be immature, volatile, and unpredictable. They can be impulsive, have higher levels of frustration, and have more difficulty making long-range plans than their peers. This creates anxiety and moments of confrontation. Fathers worry that the lack of internal discipline seen during their son's childhood will carry on into the future. Fathers often feel that because their sons were needy at the age of eight or nine, they will be so the rest of their lives.

I know my son has vast potential, the problem is seeing that potential challenged. I know he is incredibly capable, but once he starts something, you find him a few minutes later wandering off to something else. This would require that I would have to stay on him quite a bit. If I shadowed him or worked directly with him, the project would get done. If you were able to monitor him in one way or another from the beginning to completion, you know it would get done. But if you didn't, you were never sure you would get the result that was being expected. There are times that I worry what kind of man or teenager will he be. I have fears of this unruly, out-of-control kid wandering through the countryside. I know this isn't so, but I still worry when I see how unsettled he is.

◆ ◆ ◆

ADOLESCENT ISSUES

Adolescents are trying to achieve goals that frequently lead them into conflict with their environment. First, they want to be accepted by their peers, and, second, they want to separate from their parents and become more independent. While these are developmentally appropriate goals, adolescents often do not possess the tools to accomplish them without conflict. Impulsivity can impair the adolescent's ability to make decisions or to stick to a course of action. The adolescent often has problems following rules, delaying gratification, and working for larger rewards. Likewise, extra effort may be needed to inhibit behaviors or to keep from acting out. These problems may lead to confusion, to difficulties with relationships, and ultimately to poor self-concepts.

◆ ◆ ◆

I would say my son and I are not particularly close. A lot of his trouble is probably due to attention deficit. I can't say for sure, because many of my friends are having trouble with their teenagers who apparently are not ADHD. He really isn't sure what to do with his life. He started out in one four-year college, which was an academic disaster. Now he is getting ready to attend a state school, after spending a year in a local community college. In his first college, he partied a lot and was influenced heavily by his impulses.

When he was younger he had a difficult time in school and also holding onto friendships. As a teenager he is pretty moody and self-concerned. His major worry is what we are going to do for him. After bombing out of his first college, it is now up to him whether or not to pursue school. We will not pay for it anymore until he proves himself with good grades.

A few months ago I was pretty fed up with his attitude, and I mentioned the famous words of John F. Kennedy, "Ask not what your country can do for you, but rather, what you can do for your country." This was in reference to his ongoing "give me" attitude. He just shrugged his shoulders and walked away from me. At times it feels like I am seen as the "cash cow" and not much else.

My son shows no interest in being around me or involved with me. In many ways we are on two sides of a canyon with no bridge between us. I suppose a lot of this has been attributed to his ADHD. It has always been difficult for me to connect with him. His impulsivity and anger has repelled me from pursuing a close relationship.

◆ ◆ ◆

PUTTING OUT THE FIRES

In order to avoid the situation described above, fathers need a plan for resolving conflicts with their sons. In order to build

bridges and communicate without conflict, it helps to understand your own style of connecting with your son during emotional moments. ADHD can cut to the emotional core of both
the parent and the child; consequently, things are often said or
done in the heat of the moment that you later regret.

It is important to know that children usually remember what
we have done wrong and the hurtful words that we have said.
Many supportive words and moments are forgotten. This places
us in the position of defending ourselves and trying to prove
that we have been supportive or a good listener. Adolescents
also tend toward "global thinking," leading them to make state-
ments such as "You never listen to me!" "You always criticize
me!" "You are always picking on me!" "I can never do anything
right!" These situations can be held in check by understanding
and limiting your emotional response to your adolescent's behavior. The opportunity for a more reasoned approach does exist.
The following quotes from fathers indicate successful approaches
to anticipating and resolving conflicts with their sons:

Michael is a teenager. This implies that he is moving from
one stage of life to another. I know he wants nothing more
than to be successful—whether it is with his friends, at home,
in sports, or in school. Unfortunately, he is at that awkward
stage where "the directions don't always represent the finished product." What I mean is he basically knows what to
do, but when it comes to doing it, he has some problems. I
accept this, and cut him slack when it comes to getting things
done or following through. I tend to negotiate with him
about when he will do something or how he will do it. I
reconfirm what he said, and then check back after the time he
said it would get done. If it's not done, he knows I will not wait
any longer. Usually he follows through pretty well if I consult
with him rather than tell him what to do. Telling him has
never been very successful. I work very hard not to get into a
major conflict with him; this rarely is beneficial. Avoiding
the conflict is the best way to deal with conflict, in my opinion.

◆ ◆ ◆

Steve and I have worked out a system to deal with our anger or frustration. When a conflict develops, one of us, usually me, will say, "All right, things are getting the best of us. Please go ahead and say what you need to say. I will listen without interrupting you. When you are done, I will speak. Then we can exchange ideas how to best handle the situation." This works for us. This lowers the volume so we can hear each other and work on a solution. He is a teenager now. I cannot expect to force my opinion or ideas on him. Reasoning and keeping an emotional balance seems to help us.

I don't think there is any "silver bullet" for managing conflict with an adolescent. I do know that there are definitely things you want to avoid during times of conflict. Screaming, threatening, physical confrontation, sarcasm, or belittling behavior or language are all guarantees against a positive resolution. I can't say I deal with Brad the same way every time conflict surfaces. It depends on our moods and the topic at hand. I do try to keep an even keel when an argument emerges. If I maintain a level head, things are less likely to get loud or hurtful. The minute I begin raising my voice or shutting him out, we slide into a lose-lose situation.

I would say what helps us deal the best with conflict is when Ken and I keep to the issue that is causing the problem. Focusing on the issue and what is generating the problem around the issue works very well. During the times when we stray from the issue and bring up an old hurt or an old behavior, we basically shoot ourselves in the foot. Bringing up old stuff serves no purpose other than to sidetrack the issue and acknowledge that neither person has the capacity to "forgive and forget." It is amazing what staying focused on the present can do in terms of problem solving. If he took the car out three weeks ago and came home two hours late, well, that was three weeks ago. This is now. So stay in the present and let go of previous behavior. This approach builds trust and lets us remain fairly close. If I remind him of

**ADHD can bring a father to his
"emotional knees." (page 99)**

every time he did something "wrong," I wouldn't make it
to enjoy my advanced years and he would never make it out
of adolescence.

I know this may sound simple, but conflict is usually averted
when I let Jim have his say. What I mean is that I don't talk
over him, act dismissive, or talk down to him—as if I am the
alpha and the omega. It is a conversation—an exchange of
ideas and feelings. If I cut him off or he cuts me off, it
creates added tension and hard feelings. My father always
said there are two sides to a story. I express my perspective,
and I listen while Jim expresses his. After that, we assemble
a plan that will iron out the problem. Sometimes this takes
time and trust to see something through to the end, but
those are usually the times with the sweetest outcome.

◆ ◆ ◆

I use the KISS principle to resolve conflicts with Peter. You
know, Keep It Simple, Stupid (KISS). If I make things complicated or drag into the debate old news or let my anxiety

get the best of me, we are usually sunk before we launch. I make a conscious effort to sit down rather than stand up. When I stand I tend to become more animated and louder. I pay attention to my tone and the way I ask questions. If I am getting angry and I am losing perspective, I ask Peter's mother to help out with the issue. These simple things seem to work.

◆　◆　◆

PROBLEM SOLVING

Children with ADHD require a lot of time to internalize coping strategies and problem-solving skills. Adolescence in general tends to be a time of heightened urges and impulsive behaviors. This is a result of the biological and cognitive changes that are taking place. However, adolescence is also the time to allow our sons more opportunities for independent decision making and to experience the consequences of their actions. Is it possible to balance these competing needs?

The best way to characterize Michael is that he is respectful of others. I think he knows what it means to struggle and to overcome or push through difficult situations. I don't know for sure, but by some ironic means or fashion, the ADHD has shaped him into a genuinely good person. I have witnessed through the years an internal drive to succeed. He is not the brightest kid, nor is he the most talented, but I would have to say he is the most determined kid I have ever seen. He has a sense of what is right and wrong for him. Based on this, he goes after what he wants, regardless of whether other people think he can do it or not. I would say he values people's opinions, but he doesn't necessarily let others' opinions determine his decisions.

I feel much of how he responds to the world is a result of the relationship we have had throughout his formative years. I made a conscious effort to listen to him, value what he said, and in most instances let him make a choice or decision about what he should do. This is risky when you are dealing with a pretty impulsive kid. But through the years he has learned how to use reason and thoughtfulness before acting. I feel if I would have been more directive with him, he may have rebelled or chosen the opposite as an act of asserting his independence. He is very strong willed, so I decided early on that it would be more beneficial to work with him rather than demand he conform to my opinion. This type of philosophy is not easy. There were times when he would be making what I considered poor choices. The temptation was to bail him out or take control of the situation. Resisting this course has had some major payoffs.

The example above shows us that the balance can be accomplished, but how do we do it? As parents of adolescents with ADHD we need to make sure that the options and consequences are clearly stated. Adolescents must be made aware that if the privileges of adulthood are to be allowed, responsible, agreed-upon behaviors must be demonstrated. We cannot assume that our adolescents with ADHD will automatically demonstrate more responsible behavior simply because they have reached a certain age. They need to be provided the opportunity for discussion and for practicing a variety of problem-solving strategies in an atmosphere of mutual respect. This requires that parents show restraint. Adolescents definitely respond better to reaching their own conclusions based on information provided than to being told what to do or how to act. They respond much better if they are actively involved in problem-solving scenarios. Learning how to problem-solve is one of the most important tools for the future you can give your adolescent. Table 15 lists the seven steps of problem-solving.

TABLE 15

How to Problem-Solve

1. Identify the problem.

2. Generate several possible solutions.

3. Consider the consequences of each solution.

4. Choose one solution and try it.

5. Evaluate the results.

6. Consider the alternatives available if the first solution doesn't work out.

7. Try another solution until conclusion or satisfactory resolution of the problem is reached.

CONTRACTS

Because adolescents want to make their own decisions, the behavior management programs you used quite successfully when they were younger may not be as successful now. Adolescents often respond more favorably to the use of contracts. These can be used to generate agreed-upon outcomes and reinforce appropriate behaviors. The following is an example of how such a program works:

Mike has always had difficulty completing assignments. When he was in elementary school we were able to have the teacher send home his work in a folder. We would set up charts and reward him each day that he finished all his work in class and at home. In junior high this program fell apart and Mike's grades were always marked down because of "missing assignments." It was not until Mike got his driver's license that we again hit upon a plan. Together we drew up a "contract" that we all signed. It stated clearly what we expected Mike to do in order to be able to use the car at the times specified and included completing all assignments in a timely fashion. We had checks with the teachers every two weeks to see if this was done and Mike's use of the car that weekend depended on a "good" report. He could earn back the privilege of the car by completing all his work, including make-up work, over the next two-week period. Because we all contributed to drawing up the contract, and because all of the conditions were spelled out clearly, this became a very motivating tool for Mike.

BUILDING SOLID RELATIONSHIPS

I feel fortunate because, from what I either hear or see, the type of relationship some of my friends have with their teenage children is quite sad. In many respects there is almost no relationship. Many of the kids just rely on the parents for money or material things, without giving the relationship any thought. Last year Joe gave me the greatest, yet in many ways, one of the simplest compliments I could hope for. He wrote me a card on Father's Day that simply said: "No matter where I go, no matter what road I travel, or destination I find myself—I know through your example that life will be OK and I can meet my challenges head on."

Usually the strength of a father's relationship to his adolescent son is built upon the relationship that had preceded it over the years. To insure that this relationship is positive, a father must be willing to take the lead and adjust to ADHD-related behaviors. As we have said, this is not to suggest that you tolerate inappropriate behavior, but rather make a distinction between behavior that is deliberate and behavior that is impulsive and uncontrolled. The relationship then can become one of respect and mutual understanding.

My relationship with my son has always been defined by respect. We both are pretty hot tempered, so it required me to make the initial adjustment or overture in order to work out our difficulties. For Paul, the earlier developmental years were not suggestive of his using an abundance of reason in his decision making. He has generally been a fairly impulsive and emotional person. Because of this, I tried to act as the voice of reason and not get equally as excited.

Please understand, this has not been nor is it currently an easy thing to do. My Irish temper, mixed with his approach toward the world, got pretty volatile sometimes. Paul's moodiness and emotional swings were very difficult for me to deal with. With age, and a sizable amount of external and internal support throughout the years, he has learned to control his internal experience more constructively.

At 19 he is doing very well. I could go on and on about his accomplishments. Especially for a kid who his initial teachers in elementary school had very low expectations for. Early on, I think, Paul picked up on this and lived down to the expectations of his teachers. With advocacy, my wife's diligence, and my willingness to work with Paul, he is turning out to be a fine individual.

It is the amount and quality of time that is invested in these early relationships that yield results. However, quantity is not as important as quality for influencing the relationship in a positive manner. This is poignantly illustrated in the following example:

◆ ◆ ◆

Pat and I have what I consider a good relationship. He is in the midst of some interesting experiences as a teenager. We talk about how the decisions he makes now can have lasting consequences or rewards. It really is up to him and how he wants to live his life. I used to worry quite a bit about him when his mother would tell me all these things he was doing. There were times I worried about him making it in a highly competitive, technologically advanced environment. He is going to make it fine, and it will be in accordance with his own talents and interests—not necessarily the interests or expectations of those around him. This has been a significant realization for me.

I believe Pat relies on me as a sounding board when he faces important choices. I don't believe he turns to me for the answers to his difficult questions. He has gotten the message that ultimately, it's up to him to decide. My father used to say, "When you're in the water, and you're holding an oar, you have to choose which direction to row in: upstream or down. It all depends on how you want to assert your energy and what direction you want to go in." Pat has his own set of oars now. He must choose.

Since he was young, we tried to offer him every advantage possible. The one thing about Pat was, despite the moodiness or problems, he had a heart the size of Mount Everest. I think that is what my wife and I paid attention to—his heart. If we concentrated solely on his behavior, I think he would not be as self-assured as he is. Also, as rough-and-tumble a kid as he was, he had a clear tenderness and desire to do well. Because of this, I had to believe that things would turn out all right. At 18 he is a very interesting young man who has many talents, the most noticeable of which is sports.

I see many of my contemporaries having all sorts of problems with their teenage children. I think all the effort we put in on Pat and our relationship early on is paying off. Pat required time—in many ways, my time. I can't say for certain if my attention to Pat was the deciding factor in his success so far. But my wife wholeheartedly believes the time

I spent and spend with him, and the way I spend time, makes all the difference.

BUILDING A FOUNDATION

As in constructing a building where support is added one block at a time, a father's relationship with his son is built from many encounters over the years. The strength of these blocks becomes the foundation upon which other relationships are built. When the father is unavailable to his son, for whatever reason, there is often no emotional connection between the father and son. Both generally feel unappreciated and misunderstood by the other.

I would have to describe Craig as one of the most entitled kids you'll ever meet. He feels whatever he wants to do, he should be allowed to do it, without consequences. Our relationship can be described as one of tolerance: he tolerates me and I tolerate him. Our youngest son, on the other hand, who is not ADHD, is a joy to be around. I have a good relationship with him. Craig acts as if he was raised in a totally different household. I admit that I worked, and continue to work, long hours almost seven days a week. I haven't been able to give Craig my time, so I have compensated for this by showering him with material things. This has backfired in my opinion. He appreciates very little, has little respect for his mother and me, and basically does as he pleases.

This father has given up on having any relationship with his son. He feels that the level of interaction is futile and unfulfilling. It is obvious that the building blocks were loosely fitted and do not allow the father or the son to rely on one another.

Sometimes despite the best efforts of the father and the family, a son may be unable to take an active role in promoting important aspects of the relationship. The child may be unable to respond to the overtures of the family or to utilize available resources. This may result in ongoing struggles, impaired self-esteem, underachievement, and general dissatisfaction.

I have many mixed feelings about David. I think he has a lot of potential. Unfortunately, I don't see that potential being exercised very often. I think he judges himself by what he is not rather than what he could be. I think he sees himself as a rather diminished guy, with limited ability or possibilities. His brother and sister are very charismatic and bright, whereas he is best associated with a poor temperament and ongoing struggles.

Since he was young we tried to provide him with therapy and school opportunities. He never seemed to see these things as important or meaningful. Whatever we did, it never seemed to be quite enough for David. We always disappointed him at some juncture along the way. I think the most difficult thing for me in the relationship is his inability to be in the present. He seemed obsessed with what he hasn't yet done, or he wants to do more of something that is over. The present is something he slips through almost unnoticed. It is incredibly frustrating. He was diagnosed with ADHD when he was 12, kind of late, and by then I think many of the negative feelings or attitudes were entrenched. He resisted the diagnosis, medication, treatment, and the like. It has been exhausting.

REWARDING RELATIONSHIPS

As described in the following story the father of a 17-year-old sums up the benefits that can result from an ongoing effort to work with and understand a son who has ADHD. It is not always easy, it requires a great deal of effort, and the immediate results are not always apparent. However, a father's willingness to continue to learn can lead to a rewarding relationship.

My relationship with Keith is pretty good considering he is 17. He is doing very well, which is remarkable considering he has ADHD and has struggled a great deal at school and home. Up until he was around 13, his emotions would get the better of him. Let's just say he had a hard time "keeping it between the ditches." Medication gave him the opportunity to feel a great deal of success in school and at home, although I think he has resisted the idea of using medication since the first day he was placed on it. The medication let him down enough to pay attention to important details. He now uses medication only when studying for school. The other times he has learned how to control himself and how to get along in the world around him.

I am not sure how he put it all together, but he seems to be very secure now. At 17, he is able to control his behavior and outbursts—and general mood, I suppose. He uses breathing techniques, counting, removing himself from the situation, and things like this to stay on track. He seems to be doing the type of things kids his age are doing like dating, holding down a part-time job, and playing sports.

We do a lot together. He has begun to show interest in some of the things I enjoy, and I make an effort to be involved in his interests—to the degree he wants me to be. As a teenager he is spending more time with his friends and less time with us. I remember going through this transition with my family, so it feels normal to me.

The other day he gave me a great compliment by saying, "Thanks, Dad, for always being there and believing in me." I believe that's true.

◆ ◆ ◆

Chapter 9

LIVING WITH ADHD: SONS GROWN TO MEN

If you can keep your head when all about you
Are losing theirs, and blaming it on you,
If you can trust yourself when all men doubt you,
But make allowance for their doubting, too;
If you can wait and not be tired by waiting, . . .
If you can dream and not make dreams your master,
If you can think, and not make thoughts your aim,
If you can meet with triumph and disaster,
And treat those two impostors just the same . . .
Yours is the Earth and everything that's in it,
And—which is more—you'll be a Man, my Son!

Rudyard Kipling

VOICES OF YOUNG MEN

◆ ◆ ◆

I think ADHD has everything to do with who I am today. Because of the ADHD I was forced early on to examine my behavior and motivation for doing things. I assume most kids go through their childhood leaving their lives pretty much unexamined. They go to school, play sports, make friends, or whatever, and let one day merge into the next. I was lucky to have parents who realized early on that I was having some intense problems in school following directions and acting appropriately. I had testing done when i was very young, probably around five or six, and it was revealed I had ADHD and some processing difficulties. I started medication and we were involved in counseling. We still use some of the things from counseling to this day, even now that I am 21. We have family council, which is a family meeting where we discuss all sorts of issues, the good, the bad, and the ugly. My dad and I still take one day every month to do something special, and our communication is as solid as any family I know. The counseling was helpful because it didn't focus solely on me or how I was the problem. It focused on all of us and how we contributed to an outcome by certain behaviors.

◆ ◆ ◆

In this chapter we will explore the power of parenting through the stories of young adults who grew up with ADHD. Through their voices, we will discover the private thoughts and internal reality they experienced living and, in many cases, succeeding with ADHD. As we will hear, the supportive role of parents often made the difference between early success or perceived failure. Living with ADHD requires a certain fortitude and internal hardiness. It requires that the child feels supported by parents or some key adult figure. This will encourage the child

to see himself as inherently good, in spite of difficulties associated with the ADHD.

Many have described growing up with ADHD as similar to
going down hill in an out-of-control bus. The bus driver is inca-
pacitated, but there are a lot of passengers who could avert disaster by taking the wheel. You are never quite sure who or when
someone is going to take charge. For many, the medication acted
as that take-charge passenger. With maturity, the adolescent
learned to take control of the situation when the bus veered out
of control. Like the experience of the passengers on the bus, it
can be scary and tense for a child to realize that things are out of
control, but not know how to take charge. Over time and with
enough support, the adolescent and young adult with ADHD
achieves a level of balance and control that feels comfortable.
One 31-year-old man who was diagnosed with hyperactivity
when he was eight describes his experience with ADHD:

Sports were my saving grace. I knew I was good at a number
of sports, and I had a lot of positive feedback to reinforce
that belief. However, outside of sports I didn't feel very
positive about myself or my overall contributions. I have a
younger brother who is very funny and sweet, I suppose. I,
on the other hand, was moody and intense—not easy to
please and always arguing about something. I saw him re-
ceiving my parents' love and affection, while I received a lot
of "Listen, you need to control yourself" or "Leave your
brother alone" or "Pay attention" or "Try harder" or "Stop
acting that way." In many ways they were right. I think my
parents have tried to be fair and accommodating, but it was
tough with me.

As an adult I have had many talks with my father about
growing up—you know, what it was like for him and what
our relationship was like. He described me as having an incredibly big heart and trying harder than anyone he has
ever met. It's funny, but I don't really have that memory. I
have this memory or feeling of being "bad." It felt like there

were ongoing struggles between me and my parents. My mom had more patience than a saint, but it was evident when I pushed her too far. She described me as being very demanding while growing up. That feels closer to how I remember it than my dad's recollection. It's not that my dad is sugar coating it, I think that's how he wants to view me.

The one thing about my dad, and I think it was foundational in the success I have experienced in my life, is that he was always there. In every way—physically, mentally, and spiritually. He helped coach my teams, he attended my events, he sacrificed to send me to the best camps. He also had an intense belief in God, and the power that prayer can bring into a person's life. He wasn't overly religious, he was just very prayerful. I remember almost every night he would come into my room after the lights were out, hold both my hands, and spend time just remembering the day and holding in prayer the things in my heart. I think about this almost every night, still to this day.

My dad gave me time, even when he probably couldn't afford it. I miss him now. But he left me his soul, his kindness, his intensity, and his charity. I remember when I was about 13, and I did something to get in trouble in our neighborhood. When he got home from work, we went for a walk, down by the river, something we hadn't done in years. He told me a story of when he was 13, and what it was like not really having any support or anyone to talk to. He simply said, "If you ever need to talk, before you make a choice, I am here." He leaned over and kissed me on my forehead, put a twig in his mouth and leaned against a tree to watch the river rushing by. He never even mentioned the incident. That was a special moment between the two of us. I then leaned over and kissed his hand and said thanks. He smiled and put his hand on my head.

In life we have accomplished a great deal if our children remember us for our kindness and our love. These two attributes will help shape our sons into caring, dedicated men. Irrespective

**If I was getting angry I would call a time-out
using the NFL hand signals. (page 155)**

of their personality, showing loving kindness will invite our
sons to reach their potential and give back to the world around
them. They will know they are good, and it will radiate to all
those they come in contact with. When our sons feel a lack of
worthiness, that is what they convey to the world. They do not
trust and cannot be trusted. They continually find themselves
in situations that fortify their internal image of being flawed.
One man, now the father of two boys, describes what it was
like for him living with ADHD:

I constantly was in trouble growing up. I hung around the
tough kids who were pretty much unsupervised or who had
wimpy parents who didn't know what to do or didn't seem

to care. The kids I hung with had this gang mentality; we were each other's family—a chosen family that had oaths of protection and areas we supposedly dominated. I felt more at home with the wilder bunch of kids. I did what I wanted when I wanted. I honestly can't remember much about school. I don't remember studying or applying myself in school. I screwed around in class and was basically a distraction. I never felt very smart, even though people would often say how smart I was. It just never felt that way to me.

I think when I was in junior high school I had some testing done which indicated I had learning disabilities and ADD. I had to go to a reading specialist after school and other stuff. I hated it and made no bones letting my parents and the teachers know it by being a complete pain. They also recommended I go on medication for the hyperactivity. Of course, I refused that, too.

One day, it was sometime in the winter, and I was in 10th grade, I came home from skipping school for the day with my girlfriend. My dad was home, which was pretty unusual. He had some papers in his hand and told me to follow him into his bedroom. After I came in he shut the door and told me to sit down in a chair in the room. He gave me the papers and said read them. I asked all sorts of questions and he said, "For the past number of years we have had to put up with all your crap. We are no longer going to be held prisoner by you or your problems." "Read it, NOW!" he screamed. It was about a military academy in Virginia. Also inside the folder was an acceptance to the military school. I looked up in disbelief. I said, "I have to go to a military school? You're full of shit. I ain't going to any damn military school."

He said, "You've got two choices, and only two. First, you attend school every day unless you are dying of some rare disease. You do not, I repeat, do not, get below a B from now until you graduate. You go out for some high school sport, I don't give a shit which one. You ditch your so-called buds. You're in every school night by 9:00 and by

10:00 on the weekends unless we decide otherwise. Your second choice is in your hand. Certainly, there is a third choice. You can be cool and run away to live under train trestles and eat someone's dinner from the night before or splurge on canned beans. Frankly, it's up to you. But there is one thing you won't do. That is continue to live in this house and torment the family. It's over. You make your choice now. Not tomorrow or tonight. Right now."

I told my father to fuck off and threw the folder at him and split. Two days later when I came home, the locks were changed and the windows sealed. Apparently the family had gone on a week ski vacation without me. Two weeks later, I finally saw my father. I was staying with some friends, and he said if I wanted the information on the military school for me to call him at work. He said that was the only way I would be allowed back into the family. He gave me a notice from protective services saying I was a truant and a runaway and that when found I was to be remanded to juvenile hall. I felt like my life went right into a major nosedive.

A month later, I called my father at work and asked to meet with him at home. He said I could come to his office, which was 30 miles away. I said how was I supposed to get there. He said he would be in until 5:00 if I wanted to meet him. I hitched a ride out there, and it took about three hours. When I got there he'd gone home. I just sat on the steps to his office and cried like I had never cried before. The next morning I was waiting for him to arrive at work. I said I would go to the school. He gave me a train ticket and a time that evening I could come and pick up my stuff for school. I picked up my stuff that evening, and as I was leaving, he said, "If you want, you can stay here this evening, and I'll take you to the train station in the morning." His eyes were filled with tears, and I began to cry. He held me and said everything would be fine. And he was right. It was the best thing that could have happened to me.

The school taught me about me. I learned about self-direction and creating my own destiny, not having it created for me. I needed to be in that environment. I am not saying that every ADHD kid should go to military school. Not at all. But I wouldn't listen, I was getting deeper into trouble, and beginning to care less about people. Today, I am a college graduate, I have an MBA, and I am very successful in the computer industry. Oh, yeah, and my father and I are extremely close. He is a great granddad. Very caring and attentive. I wonder if he was like that as a father?

◆ ◆ ◆

Individuals with ADHD are as unique and different as snowflakes. However, all snowflakes share a similar consistency. Children with ADHD, though different in many ways, share similar attributes and attitudes. How these attributes and attitudes will turn out is dependent on the child's environment, internal resolve, and the positive messages he receives. These determine the trajectory of the ADHD and how the child grows through adolescence and into young adulthood. If the child sees himself as marred or deficient, in all likelihood he will embody these qualities in his adolescent or young adult life. Overcoming a negative disposition or attitude often takes something as dramatic as completely changing the child's environment and support structures, as in the above description of the military school.

Less dramatic shifts, toward parental consistency and support, can shore up the child's emotional belief in himself and ensure more beneficial outcomes in his life. Parental consistency, clear limits, boundaries, and anticipated consequences can prevent the type of sensational event described above. An intermediate step that families often pursue is family counseling. This allows the family to restructure communication patterns, clarify mutual goals, and create a more positive family environment. However, to achieve these things, the family as a whole must agree to work together. If one of the members is not willing to make the necessary changes, very little will be different. This is characterized in the following story:

Without question my mom and dad saw me as the problem. I was sent to a psychiatrist who specialized in difficult adolescents. After a few visits, the psychiatrist recommended we go see a family therapist. That evening my parents sat me down after school and said, "Look, this is your problem. Don't make it sound like we are the bad guys, or we all need to go to counseling together. We are spending a lot of money to send you to this psychiatrist, so figure out how you can be more productive in this family and at school. For once do something without including us." We didn't go to counseling together, and even though I tried to make changes, my parents and brother and sisters continued to treat me the same. I really couldn't catch a break from them. I remember one time in particular I was consciously trying to be different at home. My dad said, "OK, you're being nice. What do you want from us now?" That's how they saw me. As someone always trying to get over on them. I couldn't figure out how to change it. My therapist said I have to act appropriately for me and no one else. It's hard when everyone is counting on you screwing up.

◆ ◆ ◆

When individuals with ADHD experience success, it is usually because either their parents or some other adult truly believed in their ability and desire to please. When this is attended to, a child with ADHD can prosper and as a young adult can turn a disability into an asset. As one 26-year-old pharmacist summarized:

◆ ◆ ◆

My parents always said I had the potential to achieve anything I wanted. They rarely put limitations on my ability. If anything, that made the difference between me dispensing drugs legally or being on drugs illegally. School wasn't easy. Actually, very little was easy. But I kept plugging along.

◆ ◆ ◆

MOTIVATION

Motivation is a topic educators have been discussing and exploring for decades. There are people who specialize in motivational speaking or creating techniques to motivate us to enhance our performance. Motivation can refer to both the internal and external things that drive us to action.

External motivators are things like coaches, movies, or commercials. The external motivator connects with an internal desire. For instance, winning the football game. We want to win, and the coach taps into that desire by delivering a speech that gets us fired up to do our best. What is important is that the external motivator must link up with an internal desire to achieve the result. Kids are often motivated to join gangs and possibly be involved in illegal activity in order to feel a sense of belonging. The motivator is not the illegal activity initially; it is the sense of connectedness. When a commercial motivates us to buy a product to improve our bodies, we are internally motivated by a desire to change our appearance.

The purpose of this discussion is to explore what motivates children with ADHD to succeed. Possible answers may be found in the following story told by a young man who did not let the ADHD or anything else keep him from pursuing personal success:

I never really thought much about ADHD until my son was diagnosed. I had many of the same issues he has to deal with, but I probably had the kind of personality that didn't draw much negative attention my way. I went nonstop from morning until night. I had all this energy. I lettered in three sports in high school and lacrosse in college—all the while getting my schoolwork done. It was hard paying attention or focusing on schoolwork, but I was bright enough to do what I had to do to get the job done. Academics was one of my least favorite things to do, but failing or looking stupid was the ultimate disaster in my eyes. No matter what, I did not want to look stupid, even if it took me ten times longer to finish a project, I'd do it. I guess I always realized how hard school was, and that looking stupid could definitely happen, so doing whatever it took not to look stupid was my major motivator.

I am not sure where this attitude comes from, but I recall once in seventh grade not completing an assignment, and later that day the teacher had each of us get up and give a report to the class. I felt like a complete fool. Kids were snickering and jeering at me. I vowed not to feel that way again. My teacher called my mom, who relayed the story to my dad. He said, "Hey, if you need some help with school, let me know. It was not easy for me, so I'd be happy to help." That's all he said, but it made a big impact on me. I thought he was going to yell at me or ground me or something. He also said something funny, "Man, that must have been unbelievably embarrassing today. I probably would have run out of the room. Way to hang in there."

We can motivate our children. Watch, listen, and learn. They will always tell or show us what they need. Some children are gifted athletes, others are mechanically inclined, while others are academically gifted, but we must let them show us. As one young man said:

My parents let me lead the way. My dad is a famous scientist, yet he didn't force his discipline on me. I was surrounded with his passion, but not forced to embrace it. I am not scientifically inclined. He knew it, and let me choose my path. I am a lead guitarist in a pretty successful band, and I also write music. Last summer we were at the beach, and he asked me to break out my acoustic guitar and play. He fell sound asleep. That was cool.

◆ ◆ ◆

Life can be a constant uphill battle if a child feels he is a failure. As human beings, we are driven toward pursuing pleasure and avoiding or reducing pain. If we are subjected to ongoing painful experiences in our environment, we will do whatever it takes to reduce the pain and increase pleasure. Children with ADHD are more likely than non-ADHD children to pursue inappropriate peer affiliations or alcohol and other drugs in order to feel better about themselves. Ongoing negative feedback or perceived failure can drive children with ADHD toward antisocial activities. The following charts the difficult course a young man with ADHD had to navigate. Although there were many opportunities to give up or "let go of the rope," he hung on.

I haven't talked to many people who have or had ADHD, so I don't know other people's experience with it; I only know my own. When I was growing up, there weren't support groups or many parenting books and that type of thing. I sort of think my parents were flying blind when it came to dealing with me. I am not sure, but I think they thought I was an underachiever or discontented kid. I was always into something, and usually it wasn't very good. As a kid it was tough. I thought there was something wrong with me. School came hard, following rules came hard, just about everything came hard. I was the type of kid everyone would say, "If he only realized his potential." I had many talents as a kid that I never fully capitalized on.

The one thing I was aware of growing up was this impulsiveness. I wouldn't have described it as that back then, but I rarely thought things through to a logical conclusion or considered all the consequences. If I thought about it, I did it. This was true for large and small things. Buying cars or electronic equipment is a good example. I see it, I like it, I buy it. It would never occur to me to check out consumer reports or shop around for a better deal or whatever. I get this anxiousness, and have to do it right then, no matter what it is. It doesn't always work against me. There are some benefits to this. I don't get into decision-making gridlock or get confused on what to do. The downside is that I wall off a lot of options that would be better.

Because of my early experiences growing up, I have this impression of myself that I will never really amount to much. Even if I make $300,000 a year, that won't be good enough, because I'll feel like I should have done more or better. That's usually the feeling I carry around: I just don't measure up. I sort of feel my career choices have been based on taking the road of least resistance versus challenging myself academically or in other ways. I stay fairly close to my area of comfort, and travel out of that place as little as possible. I think this has limited me. Is this because of the ADHD? I don't know. I think it is related somehow. You know everyone has their own personality and their own struggles. Very few of us skip through life like Dorothy on the yellow brick road. But I do think kids that have attention deficits struggle more than others. Life is a constant tug-of-war. There is a feeling of being stuck or feeling like you can't let go for fear of falling flat on your butt.

Having ADHD makes you either resilient or walled off from the world. I have known several kids growing up who acted much like me, but their family support was almost nonexistent. This probably had a lot to do with these kids' going bad, getting in trouble a lot, and getting into drugs and booze heavily. Even though my folks were flying by the seat of their pants with me, I felt their love and support. My father was gone a lot, but when he was there, I think he supported me.

The image I get when thinking about people with ADHD is that of a prize-fighter in the ring. Life is one fighter and the person with ADHD is the other. Throughout the fight, the ADHD person has all sorts of options: give up, throw in the towel, bury his head in his gloves just to survive or minimize the pain, dance around to reduce the risk of getting hit but also reducing the possibility of getting in some good licks, or fighting until he hears the bell. Once he hears the bell he goes to his corner where his support is, where people can guide him in how to keep going and lick the other fighter.

The corner is a respite, it's time-out from the battle. I want to believe that I have been going until I hear the bell. There have been times that I have thrown in the towel, but fortunately they have been few. People with ADHD can get beat up a lot. No one likes to take it on the chin, but this ADHD leaves kids few options. I think they have the potential to lose a lot. Having a good support system like the coach in the fighter's corner can make a huge difference.

◆ ◆ ◆

THE ROLE OF TEMPERAMENT

Temperament plays an important role in the father-son relationship, determining its strength and quality. When the father and son both have volatile temperaments, their interactions are frequently fraught with tension and despair. When a child has a high-impact temperament and is hard to please or extremely demanding, this must be balanced with an equal amount of calm. A father's or mother's rage only serves to heighten the child's anxiety and intensity.

Jim Tunney, an official in the NFL, describes anger management in this way: "I learned a long time ago that you can't deal with anger by using anger. You've got to deal with coolness, with a feeling of being unperturbed. Inside I might be very angry, but I'm not going to let that person know he has controlled my behavior. Why should I let somebody else control me?" Controlling one's immediate reaction to someone else's behavior requires a great deal of self-discipline and the belief that remaining calm will achieve the desired result. If we allow ourselves to get swept away by the moment, the result is usually escalation of the problem.

The following exemplifies the importance of the parent remaining calm:

My dad was very laid back. Even when I would be all over the place, he rarely seemed to get real upset with me and blow up. My mom was more of a screamer and hothead like me. When my mom got wound up, Dad would show up and usher me away to do something with him. His calm nature allowed me to calm down and get a healthier perspective on the situation. We attended family therapy for a while, and the therapist pointed out that my mother and I were similar in temperament. When we got angry, it was red hot. He suggested some ways my mother and I could handle our anger differently. We both agreed to try different ways of handling our emotions. For the most part I would say it worked.

If I was getting angry I would literally call a time-out, you know, use the NFL hand signals and everything. This would tell her that I was beginning to boil. She would take a deep breath and think for a moment and approach me differently. She would slow me down by gently putting her hands on the top of my head to indicate I was getting overheated. These type of things sound stupid, but they were effective in helping us relate better to each other. Most importantly, it taught me a lot about my temper and how destructive it can become if I let it. This has been very helpful for me as a father. If I get angry with the kids, I have devised these tricks with them to slow the situation down and get a better perspective.

Having ADHD can be a wonderful gift. As described below, this father of two girls considers his ADHD to be a blessing of sorts. Amidst the difficulty, something unique and special has emerged. For many, living with ADHD can be a burden, but as described below it can unearth hidden gifts. Not taking things for granted and working toward personal discipline are just two of the gifts that can accompany ADHD.

It's funny, when I think about my childhood I can't really remember much. This has always bothered me. A therapist

I once saw stated this isn't uncommon for someone with ADHD. She said we tend to be so preoccupied with events and distracted that the moment slips away, many times unnoticed. This makes sense to me, but it is also sad. It's like accidentally erasing your hard drive on your computer. You don't have a back up, and the C drive had all your important documents spanning decades. It's sad, that's all.

As an adult and a father, I can now say that the ADHD has been a benefit. I am a fairly empathic person, who is very people oriented—unlike my brother, who is a real technical guy with limited people skills. He was the bookworm and intense jock, while I was very social and somewhat academically marginal. Like my parents at times, I think my brother saw me as basically unmotivated or lazy. Even though we are close in age, we had very little in common, and shared friends rarely.

As an adult, I have spent a great deal of time learning to become more disciplined and organized, two things I was definitely not growing up. Therapy, support groups, and reading have given me some clear direction in how to live the most productive life I can. I also work very hard as a father. My daughters are not ADHD, or at least I don't think they are. I spend a lot of time with them and try to treat them with respect, regardless of what's happening.

◆ ◆ ◆

OUTCOMES

It is important to realize that individuals with ADHD are often aware of their inappropriate behavior as it is occurring. But like the deer caught in the headlights, a paralysis occurs preventing them from immediately altering the course of their actions. Thoughtful consideration of actions or behaviors develops as the child grows older. This process can be accelerated with outside support such as therapy or team sports. Outside assistance helps offset a lot of negative self-talk many children with ADHD engage in. These messages can take the form of "I am stupid" or "I should kill myself to make everyone happy" or "No one really loves me in this family" or "The family would be better off without me."

Young adults who experienced some form of consistent external assistance generally report having a fairly robust self-image.

◆ ◆ ◆

I have been on medication since I can remember. I seriously cannot remember not having to take it. From what I gather, I was diagnosed with ADHD when I was around four. My parents say that I was in three preschools before they had me diagnosed. I have memories of being eight or nine and my parents saying, "OK, we want you to take control today without the medicine." This was usually a disaster until I was older. I really couldn't hold it together. My parents would get angry at me and start fighting between the two of them. I know they really hoped I could do it without my medicine.

When I wasn't on medication, I was all over the place. I mean like a hose whirling around the ground under high pressure. On medicine I was in control, thoughtful, patient, remorseful, etc. Off medicine I was tough to be around. And I knew it just as well as my parents or brothers. I knew I wasn't doing the "right thing," but I just couldn't stay on track. I also didn't have the words or insight to understand or describe the way I do now.

My dad would say, "This is all I expect, just keep your hands off other people and treat others with respect. I don't want to keep you from having fun or being a kid, I just want you to act appropriately." I heard the words, but shortly thereafter I was screaming, or grabbing, or bothering someone. I seriously wanted to die at a young age because I realized how much people didn't want to be around me.

I still feel bad at times and the impulse to do something inappropriate is there. Fortunately, I have learned strategies to control it. I consciously pull away from a situation, take some deep breaths, and think about what I need to do. My attention span is longer now, and I can accomplish what I need to and keep moving toward my personal goals. Therapy helped a lot, along with a better relationship with my family. They have had to put up with a lot from me. I realize it and appreciate it. I also know that change has to begin and end with me. For years I expected everyone else to change in order to be happy. Finally at 26, I have figured out where happiness exists for me—it is inside me, not in something or someone.

◆ ◆ ◆

Dag Hammerskjold said, "There is a point at which everything becomes simple and there is no longer any question of choice, because all you have staked will be lost if you look back. Life's point of no return." There is a point in everyone's life when they must choose how to live. This choice will often be determined by patterns of behavior that have developed over time. If the behaviors are negative, such as stealing, lying, or substance abuse, it may be very difficult for a person to redirect them as he moves through adolescence and into young adulthood. Consequently, the earlier the intervention, the better.

IN HIS OWN TIME

In their book, *Raising a Son: Parents and the Making of a Healthy Man,* Don and Jeanne Elium discuss the concept of a child's personal readiness for change in this way: "No matter how hard we push, cajole, or pray, his soul will move him onward only when it is ready, and when his, not our, conditions are right. There is no way to calculate when that moment will be, but we will have no doubt that it has happened." We can certainly create a loving, supportive, and nurturing environment for our children, but they must choose how to use the resources made available to them. There is a saying, "We can't make our

**I was like a hose whirling around
under high pressure. (157)**

children do anything other than rebel." We can force them with threats to act a particular way, but inevitably this has a way of backfiring on both the child and parent. Giving him the room to follow his own course is a tremendous gift we can offer our child. We must believe that if we are doing all we can to support our child, at some point we must let him assume responsibility for himself. The following brings this concept into sharper focus:

◆   ◆   ◆

My dad especially wanted me to be this great football player, like he was in college. He would always say how much talent I had, and how I was pissing it away by not paying attention or listening to the coaches. He would be at every practice, yelling at me, giving me the silent treatment on the way home if I didn't live up to his expectations. I hated it, and now that I am a father I will never do that to my son. When I told my father that I was not going to play college ball, you would have thought I told him I was just accused of murder. He said someday I would regret my laziness and self-centeredness. If I wanted to go to college I would have to pay for it. My feeling is that he wanted me to be someone I am not, or someone he was not. The only thing I can remember him wanting to do with me was throw the football around. That was our relationship. When I chucked football to pursue my own interests, that relationship, as it were, was over.

In this example, the father was pushing his son beyond the son's desire to play football. Regardless of the child's ability level, he did not feel the same way about football as his father. The father may have believed that the harder he pushed the more the son would grow to accept his ideas.

There are certain things our children must do whether they like it or not, such as chores around the house. While children would rather be playing or doing anything else, as a member of a family, they should be responsible to contribute to the needs of the household. Parental modeling of doing chores is essential. One young father who has three children stated:

I always saw my father doing chores and helping out around the house. He would always contribute to the maintenance of the house. He was famous for answering our question "When will I be done?" with "When I am finished." He was always right there helping and doing his part.

Children may not like housework, but it is reasonable that we insist they do it. It is when we push our hopes and dreams onto an unwilling child that we risk damaging the relationship and, in some instances, the child.

I really saw my father as a tyrant. I didn't enjoy being around him, and honestly gave very little weight to what he said or did. My grades were never like my sister's, or my commitment never as strong as my brothers', and on and on. He gave me crap constantly. Once we were at this large community picnic, and a dad came up to my father and praised me as this really neat kid who was very helpful. My dad looked at me and said, "You can't be talking about this kid. If he's so great with you, you can have him." He was dead serious. The other dad kind of made this nervous laugh, touched me on the shoulder, and walked away. My father frequently would say that I used my disability, my ADHD, as an excuse for not doing my best. He would say that I hid behind it because I was afraid to take risks.

My mom understood the ADHD, and she understood me. It's really because of her that I have turned out to be a productive man and committed father. My father is who he is. I spend very little time thinking about him or his ways. I concentrate on what I need to do to be successful in my life. We are cordial with one another. I share virtually no information with him. I think now he really feels that. Especially with my children. I don't encourage them to have a relationship with my father, and we visit my parents infrequently. My mother flies down for two weeks a year, and the kids love when she's here. I see my father maybe once or twice a year, which is fine. It's unfortunate, though. He missed out on a lot with me; now he is missing it with his grandchildren. I did my best you know; I really did my best.

Encouraging our children to follow their own path has enormous benefits. To do this we have to remind ourselves at the moment when we want to push or even berate our child that he is doing the best he can. It certainly may not seem like it to us, but he is either out of control or in the throws of a difficult emotional experience. How we respond to him at that moment is critical, and can make the difference between him feeling failure or the opportunity for success. The words we speak to our children are powerful and frequently remembered by them long after we have forgotten the interaction.

This may be true for all children, regardless of whether they have ADHD or some other problem. But I always remembered the negative things my father said to me. He was a great dad, but when he got fed up he would say things like, "You really are worthless" or "The only person you even remotely care or think about is yourself." I remember these things. I remember they would hit me hard. I also remember dealing with the hurt of it by getting angry at him or defiant. But it hurt. I can't be sure, but he was probably trying to shame me out of the behavior. I now see my oldest son, who has ADHD, doing the type of things I must have done, and there is a part of me that now understands how he felt. There are times against my better judgment, when I catch myself saying similar things to my son. This is one tradition I do not want to carry on.

Fathers are human. We lose our temper, say things we regret, or even do things we regret. Fortunately, our children have an enviable ability to forgive. We can express our humanity through reaching out and saying simply, "I am sorry" or "What I did was inappropriate; I lost my temper. I'll work hard to avoid doing that again." When we acknowledge our behavior, good or bad, we model for our children that it is appropriate to recognize how we affect and influence people in our lives. At times, what we do in response to a particular behavior can seem harsh and punitive. The following story reminds us that to forgive is divine, and to ask for forgiveness often takes courage:

A number of thoughts enter my mind, but when I think of my dad, I think of the times he held me and said he was sorry for what he said or did. I would say, "It's OK, Dad," and he would say, "No, no, it's not OK to treat you or anyone like I just did. You can't help it sometimes, and I tend to forget that." My mom tells me that he would try all sorts of ways to deal with the situation before losing it. Once he became angry, he would really get angry. My mom also said I was a tough kid to deal with. I had a bad temper and had a hard time completing anything. If I didn't get my way, I was inconsolable. That's what my dad to this day says was the most difficult thing for him to deal with. As tough as my dad was, he was also a very gentle man who didn't mind showing his feelings or certainly admitting when he did something wrong. I think that attitude took a certain amount of courage. Sort of admitting weakness to your children. I think partly that's what has made me so strong.

◆ ◆ ◆

Chapter 10

CONCLUSION

Without question, parents are the most influential models in a child's early years. Parents have the opportunity to show their children the most appropriate ways to get specific needs met. The following story encourages parents to advocate for their children regardless of what others (including the school system) may feel about the child or his disability:

Little Ken has special needs. So both my wife and I know we have to stick up for Ken, and we can't take anything for granted, such as expecting that the teachers will understand his special needs or treat him in a respectful way. But to get the resources that will help Ken, we really have had to be prepared to be the noisy gong to get his needs met. My wife and I want to model for Ken that if you need something, there is an appropriate way to get it, and not to let other people's opinions stop you or discourage you.

ADHD can be taxing and require a significant amount of effort by the parent. It can, additionally, be a positive force for bringing a father and son closer together. The following describes a father's appreciation of the ADHD for creating the opportunity for him to have had a positive influence in his son's life:

I think the ADHD has allowed Josh and me to get closer than we may have if he didn't have difficulties. I may have taken for granted his successes and not concentrated on them as much. It has created the opportunity for us to grow closer and to communicate more than if he didn't have ADHD. I now spend more time with Josh than with my other two children, because they seem more self-sufficient and require my attention less. I think my involvement has allowed Josh to feel better about himself and has helped in his personal control in the family.

One father describes how he stepped back and allowed his son freedom of expression and relied on his son's behavior to signal what type of support was welcome. This takes a great deal of patience and acceptance by the father.

After we learned that Steve was ADHD, I wanted some type of definitive test that would tell us that he has this disorder. But there is no blood test or magical questionnaire that will say he has ADHD. The only way we and others can know for sure that he has ADHD is through his behavior. His behavior indicates what he can and cannot, for now, do. He has some developmental delays and also struggles with certain learning disabilities. What this says to me is that I cannot compare his development to that of some other six-year-old kid. I have to let Steve lead the way and let us know behaviorally what he can handle. Since he is so young, he cannot verbally express his frustration. His frustration right now comes out in his behavior. Although it took me a while to realize this, I now look to his behavior to signal what my appropriate response should be, rather than demand he fit into my goals and desires. I focus on what Steve can do and I try to challenge him at that level. I praise his accomplishments, regardless of what they may be, and try to subtly challenge him to reach a little farther than his grasp.

IT ALL TAKES TIME

Providing your child with the appropriate level of support and intervention does not mean that his behavior will change immediately. It may take time for him to believe that behavior change is possible. The response of the parent to the child is a major factor in how quickly he begins to adopt more positive coping strategies. Positive reinforcement and supportive responses, even when your child is in a bad mood, are what seem to create the greatest gains. Being a positive cheerleader for your son may also allow him to accept more challenges and try new activities.

I do not focus on my son's problems very often, and I am careful not to use language that will force him to look at his deficits. I mean like saying, "Why can't you pay attention for once?" You know, that kind of thing. It's not always easy, but I think calling out the positive stuff dodges a bunch of problems. It also sets him up to take on more positive challenges and try out new things. If he thought that I was going to criticize him all the time, I don't think he would be quite so adventurous and outgoing.

FOCUSING ON THE POSITIVE

When a father chooses not to focus on his child's deficits, both the father and son experience tremendous gains in the relationship. The father feels a sense of positive feedback and optimism, while the son continues to thrive and strive. The positive focus by the father also creates an emotionally safe environment for the child.

It doesn't do any good to stay in the hand-wringing stage regarding ADHD. I hear about a lot of parents who really expend large amounts of energy concentrating on what their kids are not doing well. I also think it is easy to do that because these kids present so many problems. I try to focus on what my son is doing right. Granted he is in the next second doing something inappropriate, but I try not to focus on that. I see lots of gains from Chad when he feels I am on the same team with him versus being the opponent.

This process of honoring a child's abilities creates a personal freedom for both the child and the parents.

My objective for my son is to make sure, as much as I can, that he experiences successes. That is really the bottom line. We are part of the school of thought that believes in a child having a fulfilled life. We want to support him in finding his fulfillment through home and wholesome activities that leave him feeling good.

LEARNING MORE ABOUT YOURSELF

ADHD is most usually genetic in origin and consequently many fathers recognize vestiges of the same behaviors in themselves that they see in their sons. At times, this can make it more difficult to connect with or support your son, but on the other hand, it can provide you with a great deal more empathy.

Often, however, fathers need to assess themselves and look at their background before they can offer help to their child. This can sometimes be an extremely difficult task.

> When I look at my son, I am sure that many of his current struggles are very similar to struggles I encountered. I also find myself being harsher on him when he displays characteristics or traits that I also have, so I try to shake them out of him, sometimes literally. My son is an extension of me— be that good, bad, or indifferent. I must assume responsibility for my role in modeling behavior for him and helping him accept parts of himself that are not terribly flattering. I have learned that before I can really help my son, I have to look at my own behaviors and responses to the world. That has not been an easy place to start.

Be a positive cheerleader for your son. (page 166)

Often children with ADHD offer fathers the opportunity to heal historical wounds stemming from their own ADHD. Much of the healing can come through either offering their son the support that was lacking when they were younger or establishing healthy ways for the family to deal with issues related to the ADHD.

Unquestionably it is like history repeating itself in terms of what Rob is going through. What he is going through is uncomfortably close to what I experienced. What people say to him, including me, is the same thing that they said to me, "You are so bright. Why don't you apply yourself?" Now that I am going through this experience with Robbey, I am able to sift through my own experiences and put a lot of it to rest. It's also helpful that I can do some healing by being there for him in a way that I didn't receive help.

◆ ◆ ◆

In the following passage a father recognizes that by being aware of and involved in his son's life, he may help his son to avoid some of the academic struggles that he had while growing up. Although school was hard for the father, he did not feel his parents were involved as much as he would have liked. Because the father has a strong memory of what it was like for him, he intends to encourage his son in his academic pursuits.

◆ ◆ ◆

If I were to really be honest with myself, I would have to say that I had or have ADHD. I was never very good at focusing and that type of thing. I probably had this all along and was never diagnosed. I was a good athlete and received a lot of praise and reinforcement that way, and I conned my way through school. I was real social. I was always a popular type kid in school. I just did the bare minimum to get by. The place I really excelled was on the athletic field. I could cut loose there with impunity. I did whatever I needed to do to get by without the teachers giving me a hard time. I don't want to see Seth do this, but I feel I am more involved than my folks were. Plus I know what to do in terms of him trying to coast. I believe, probably with more encouragement, or a belief that I could do more, I would have done better. I got a lot of "You're lazy" or "You don't try."

◆ ◆ ◆

Thus, being the father of a child with ADHD creates the opportunity for the father to learn more about himself and his role as a parent.

◆ ◆ ◆

In reflecting on my relationship with Todd, it is hard to know what to associate with general parenthood and what to associate with being the parent of an ADHD child. I realize that I am not as patient a person as I thought I was. That would probably be true even without an ADHD child, but I think that Todd's having ADHD has made this much clearer. Todd has allowed me to learn the true meaning of patience and, to a degree, tolerance. I have had to learn how to hold my child when my first instinct would be to yell or walk away. This has been the greatest lesson for me: that when I meet him where he is developmentally, he comes out of it, although not right away, with a sense that he is okay and that struggles are a part of life. His own growth and courage have made me stretch in ways I probably would not have chosen to stretch as a parent. The ADHD has permitted me to confront certain aspects of my own perceived limitations as a father and a man.

◆ ◆ ◆

SUPPORT FOR YOURSELF

You *can* provide the love, energy, and support your children with ADHD need, but it takes work and our consistently being there. However, in order to keep giving, you also need to receive support yourself. This book is meant to give you some of that support and provide you with insight and information for choosing the most appropriate path to travel with your son.

EPILOGUE

VOICES FROM GRANDFATHERHOOD

Following are the reflections of a 65-year-old father whose 38-year-old son struggled with ADHD into adulthood. Now as a grandfather, he is witnessing his nine-year-old grandson having to confront many of the same ADHD-related issues.

My earliest memories of my son, during the early years, before he began school, involve seeing this kid running around like a loose cannon. He would inevitably be the kid at the top of the highest tree, or holding the BB gun after a window was shot out, or getting in some sort of trouble in the neighborhood. He was this little fearless wild-man at the ages of 3, 4, and 5. In many ways, he was the ballsiest little kid I had ever seen. This type of "leading with his chin" tended to keep him under a lot of scrutiny—both by us and the neighbors. If he wasn't taking the heat for something he did, then he was taking the heat for someone else. He was "full of piss and vinegar," as the old saying goes.

Even though he had a lot of misplaced energy, I always thought my son was an interesting kid. He wasn't a dull child. He did interesting things and made interesting observations. His energy level was very different from mine, so it was intriguing to see him operate in the world. I enjoyed the hell out of him. There was a certain degree of hand-wringing when disciplining measures didn't work, but, by and large, he was a joy to be around.

From another perspective, I always found my younger brother to be equally as interesting. Both my brother and my son have similar personalities—charismatic, funny, hell-bent for freedom, the first to try something zany. I honestly never worried about how he would turn out as he got older or what kind of man he would be. I worried about him because I had visions of him going over Niagara Falls in a barrel, but I didn't worry about his future—what he would become. On a day-to-day level I was concerned about him, but I wasn't consumed by a fear that he would be socially rejected or miss having a full life. I knew, intuitively, that he would be productive and make a contribution to his community and the world in his own way. Although I know he had problems, I never saw him as disabled, limited, or incapable. I never felt this way about him, so I never conveyed this image to him. Granted he had problems, but who doesn't?

And I feel the same way about my grandson, Paul, who has many of the same characteristics and struggles as his father. I intuitively know he will do enormously well in this world, and this world will be a better place because of him. I am not trying to paint a rosy picture of what awaits Paul. Having ADHD, I have learned, is very difficult and can present many obstacles. I have witnessed, however, my son struggle with similar issues and achieve enormous success. If they were taking odds in Vegas 30 years ago, the odds would have been against him.

I remember getting caught up in my son's problems, pounding the table, taking away privileges, and making countless threats in an attempt to change his behavior. And there were also moments of despair. Yet, amidst it all there was never a loss of hope or pride in the fact that he was my son. I know this may sound like some post hoc dramatization of how I felt, but this was an awareness that I carried every day of my son's life.

Since my outlook on things and my chemistry were so different from my son's, I could view his behavior and the situations he got into with a certain amount of intrigue and emotional distance. Unfortunately, and maybe unfortunately is the incorrect word here, my son and his son have a very similar chemistry, which seems to cause a great deal of friction and intensity between the two. It seems to me that my grandson has been labeled very early. I never really viewed my son as disabled, yet I see that label being affixed to my grandson. There is an element of sadness when I think about this. The difference is that my son was labeled by the community and not me; my grandson has been labeled by his father and not the community. My son is very caught up in the negative aspects of Paul's ADHD.

While both my son and his wife have been very involved and responsive to Paul's needs since he has been very young, I think this attention has been a both a blessing and a curse. It is a blessing because little Paul was definitely struggling when his parents began pursuing answers to his difficulties. It is a curse because his troubles have become all consuming. His behavior and overall presentation to the world is constantly being examined. I remember being concerned about my son's behavior, but not consumed. My grandson, on the other hand, always seems to be in a test tube in terms of his behavior. He is constantly being observed and scrutinized. I considered what was going on with my son when he was growing up as being part of his makeup, you know, like having brown eyes or a "ballsy" attitude. It was just him. I could help him manage his world, but I wasn't going to try to control it for him.

I am not saying that I was a better father than my son is now. He and his wife work hard to provide a loving and attentive home for each other and their children. What I am saying is that his parents' being too involved or overinvolved might stifle some of Paul's inner yearnings or creativity. This may be limiting in terms of what he can ultimately accomplish. Day-to-day living cannot be a laboratory, and I wonder if little Paul doesn't spend a great deal of time in his father's laboratory. But I don't know this for certain. I am mentioning it because it needs to be considered.

I know in raising my son I got a tremendous amount of joy out of watching him and being around him. Other than baseball, I don't know if my son enjoys the time he spends with Paul. When they are around each other they interact with a series of command–response–command–response. There is not much real talking. I don't know if their relationship is like this all the time or not; I would suspect it is probably a fair representation of what goes on in the relationship. I see my son so worried about how Paul will "turn out" later in life that he misses who his son is right now. Again, this is my observation.

My son clearly seems to have a different relationship with all his children. He seems to enjoy the second oldest, who has a carefree, more independent spirit, much more. He comes and goes and has a much lighter, less intense relationship with his father than Paul does. I also think this troubles Paul. I think he would like that type of relationship, but he doesn't know how to get it. My son, I know, wishes he could have a more relaxed relationship with Paul. When Paul and his dad are in the same vicinity, they create this intense magnetic field. This creates a situation where they are always in each other's gravitational pull. They want to break free, yet seem unable to.

I don't want to overdramatize this, but there is an attraction; Paul and his dad share a mutual need to be around one another. Paul really wants to be around his dad, but he is not sure how to navigate the terrain of the relationship. He's got the map but not the compass, or vice versa. Paul is at an age now where he could go out and perform on his own and come back and report to his father about his accomplishments or his performance. This would encourage Paul to become more self-sufficient without having to always be under the watchful eye of his father. Sort of like replicating his school performance. He goes to school and then comes home to report how it went. I think this type of interaction would give him more confidence in what he is doing and thinking. There is a point where he must learn to stand on his own and live with his choices.

When I see Paul and his dad engaged in an intense interaction, my instinct is to say, "Hey, just reason with him, he'll get it." I know this is easier said than done. I am not saying their interaction is spontaneous combustion. My son does try to work with Paul, but this quickly turns to frustration and anger when Paul falls short of the expected response or behavior. I desperately want to intervene to break the cycle of tension, but I don't know how I would do that or if it would be appropriate. I want to take Paul out of the situation and go for a walk to help him and his father gain a calmer perspective.

I remember when my son got in trouble, it wasn't cataclysmic. He handled his problems with solid responses. I was always proud to see him assume responsibility for his behavior. He always wanted to participate in resolving the problem. This was tangible evidence that I was participating in his growth, in shaping him for his future life as an adult. I wasn't really a disciplinarian; I was more of a coach. I suppose I don't see young Paul as capable of or as willing to deal with his problems the way my son was. I see Paul less willing to assume accountability for his behavior. I remember my son getting in all sorts of situations, but I don't remember him shirking his responsibility when he did something good or bad. He would take the blame when it was justified, and at times when it was not.

I am prone to take the perspective that we all have mountains to climb and difficulties to surmount during the course of our lifetime. As human beings we are flawed. So we all have some type of flaw that can potentially hinder us in our growth and accomplishments. Some flaws, like ADHD, are just more glaring than others. The key is to figure out how to parlay our problems into advantages. My son didn't let ADHD sideline him from enjoying life and being successful. Paul, in a large sense, is fortunate that his flaw is correctable and manageable and can be transformed into something quite astounding.

This is where I think the type of support and nurturance my son gives Paul will pay off in spades. As much as the relationship is intense, Paul knows he is deeply loved and cherished, and basically he has gotten the message that he can accomplish anything he wants. I believe Paul will come out way ahead of his peers who have not had to address the type of issues he has had to deal with.

I see my grandson's struggles as no different from most kids his age. He is trying to find himself—find out who he is. At times, he is working against his father to figure this stuff out. Maybe this is natural. I don't know because I didn't grow up with a father, so I have no real way to judge. I do see my son being as involved today with Paul as he was five years ago. I think there should be some letting go, some loosening of the reins, some release. I think this is necessary to allow the beginning of real maturity. Maybe I am looking for it too soon, may be it's not time to give him some room. Intuitively, it feels to me like it is time to relax and let him lead more in making decisions.

I think developing a resilient child minimally requires a belief in the child's inherent goodness and providing that child with a solid structure and home life. I believe that is what I did for my son and my son is now doing for his children, especially Paul. Either we define what type of culture and values we want our children to live with, or the larger culture will define our childrens' values for them. I see my son and his wife being the rock that their children lean on and retreat to when the larger culture becomes overwhelming. If your children do not have this, you run the risk of someone outside the family defining their values for them. I believe our children are heavily influenced by what we do or do not do. Whether we like it or not, whatever we do, we model that behavior for our children.

I have to say that my son lives with what I call integrity. I mean he displays an honesty to his children that invites their feedback, even during times when he would rather not hear it. This openness allows them to have a voice and a place of meaning in the family. This also is what my wife and I tried to give our children. Basically it all boils down to love. I believe my grandchildren feel loved as my son felt loved by us. My son is carrying on a very important tradition.

RESOURCES

BOOKS FOR CHILDREN

On ADHD

Distant Drums, Different Drummers, Barbara Ingersoll, 1995, Bethesda, MD, Cape Publications, 32 pages, $15.95.

Eagle Eyes: A Child's View of Attention Deficit Disorder, Jeanne Gehret, 1991, Fairport, NY, Verbal Images Press, 32 pages, $9.95.

Learning to Slow Down and Pay Attention, 2nd edition, Kathleen Nadeau and Ellen Dixon, 1997, New York, Magination Press, 80 pages, $10.95.

Otto Learns About His Medicine, Matthew Galvin, 1988, New York, Magination Press, 32 pages, $9.95.

Putting on the Brakes: Young People's Guide to Understanding Attention Deficit Disorder (ADHD), Patricia Quinn and Judith Stern, 1991, New York, Magination Press, 64 pages, $9.95.

The "Putting on the Brakes" Activity Book for Young People with ADHD, Patricia Quinn and Judith Stern, 1993, New York, Magination Press, 88 pages, $14.95.

On Problem-Solving

What Do You Think? A Kid's Guide to Dealing with Daily Dilemmas, Linda Schwartz, 1993, Santa Barbara, CA, Learning Works, 184 pages, $9.95.
What Would You Do? A Kid's Guide to Tricky and Sticky Situations, by Linda Schwartz, 1990, Santa Barbara, CA, Learning Works, 184 pages, $9.95.

On Self-Esteem

Just Because I Am: A Child's Book of Affirmations, Lauren Murphy Paine, 1994, Minneapolis, Free Spirit Publishers, 32 pages, $6.95.
Marvelous Me, Linda Schwartz, 1979, Santa Barbara, CA, Learning Works, 32 pages, $3.95.
Self-Esteem: A Classroom Affair, Volumes I and II, Michelle and Craig Borba, 1978 and 1982, San Francisco, HarperCollins, 144 pages each, $14.00 each.

BOOKS FOR ADOLESCENTS

On ADHD

ADD and the College Student: A Guide for High School and College Students with Attention Deficit Disorder, edited by Patricia O. Quinn, New York, Magination Press, 128 pages, $13.95.
ADHD: A Teenager's Guide, James Crist, 1996, King of Prussia, PA, Center for Applied Psychology, 176 pages, $27.95.
Adolescents and ADD: Gaining the Advantage, Patricia O. Quinn, 1995, New York, Magination Press, 88 pages, $12.95.
I Would If I Could: A Teenager's Guide to ADHD/Hyperactivity,

Michael Gordon, DeWitt, NY, GSI Publications, 34 pages, $10.00.

Making the Grade: An Adolescent's Struggle with ADD, Roberta Parker, available from A.D.D.Warehouse, 800-233-9273, 47 pages, $10.00.

School Strategies for ADD Teens, Kathleen Nadeau, Ellen Dixon, and Susan Biggs, Chesapeake Psychological Publications, 5041 A&B Backlick Road, Annandale, Virginia 22003, 703-642-6697, 58 pages, $7.95.

On School Success

Get Off My Brain: Survival Guide for Lazy Students, Randall McCutcheon, 1985, Minneapolis, Free Spirit Publishing, 120 pages, $8.95.

How to Be School Smart: Secrets of Successful Schoolwork, Elizabeth James and Carol Barkin, 1988, New York, Lothrop, Lee and Shepard Books, 96 pages, $6.95.

On Relationships

Bringing Up Parents: The Teenager's Handbook, Alex J. Parker, Minneapolis, Free Spirit Publishing, 276 pages, $12.95.

BOOKS FOR PARENTS AND PROFESSIONALS

On ADHD

Attention Deficit Disorder: Diagnosis and Treatment from Infancy to Adulthood, Patricia O. Quinn, 1996, New York, Brunner/Mazel, 240 pages, $23.95.

Attention Deficit Hyperactivity Disorder: A Clinical Workbook,

Russell Barkley, 1991, New York, Guilford Press, 112 pages, $25.00.

Attention-Deficit Hyperactivity Disorder: Handbook for Diagnosis and Treatment, Russell Barkley, 1990, New York, Guiford Press, 747 pages, $50.00.

Attention Deficit Hyperactivity Disorder: Questions and Answers for Parents, Gregory S. Greensberg and Wade F. Horn, 1991, Champaign, IL, Research Press, 144 pages, $12.95.

Driven to Distraction: Recognizing and Coping with Attention Deficit Disorder from Childhood through Adulthood, Edward Hallowell and John Ratey, 1994, New York, Pantheon Books, 319 pages, $23.00.

Hyperactive Children Grown Up: ADHD in Children, Adolescents, and Adults, 2nd edition, Gabrielle Weiss and Lily Hechtman, 1993, New York, Guilford Press, 473 pages, $19.95.

Managing Attention Deficit Disorders in Children: A Guide for Practitioners, Sam Goldstein and Michael Goldstein, 1990, New York, John Wiley & Sons, 451 pages, $52.00.

Taking Charge of ADHD: The Complete Authoritative Guide for Parents, Russell Barkley, 1995, New York, Guilford Press, 294 pages, $16.95.

When You Worry About the Child You Love, Edward Hallowell, 1996, New York, Simon & Schuster, 280 pages, $23.00.

On Adolescents

ADHD and Teens: A Parent's Guide to Making It Through the Tough Years, Colleen Alexander- Roberts, 1995, Dallas, Taylor, 208 pages, $12.95.

Surviving Your Adolescents, Thomas Phelan, Glen Ellyn, IL, Child Management, 136 pages, $12.95.

Teenagers with ADD: A Parents' Guide, Chris Dendy, Rockville, MD, Woodbine House, 400 pages, $16.95.

On Behavior Management

One-Two-Three Magic: Training Your Childen to Do What You Want!, 2nd edition, Thomas Phelan, 1995, Glen Ellyn, IL, Child Management, 192 pages, $10.00.

On Fatherhood

Fatherhood, Bill Cosby, 1987, Berkeley, CA, Berkeley Books, 178 pages, $6.95.

Fathering: Strengthening Connection with Your Child No Matter Where You Are, Will Glennon, 1995, Berkeley, CA, Corari Press, 219 pages, $10.95.

Raising a Son: Parents and the Making of a Healthy Man, Don and Jeanne Elium, 1992, Hillsboro, OR, Beyond Words Publishing, 244 pages, $12.95.

ORGANIZATIONS

ADDA, The National Attention Deficit Disorder Association, 9930 Johhnycake Ridge, Suite 3E, Mentor, OH 44060; 216-350-9595; 216-350-0223 (fax).

CH.A.D.D., Children and Adults with Attention Deficit Disorder, National Office, 499 N.W. 70th Avenue, Suite 101, Plantation, FL 33317; 954-587-3700; 954-587-4599 (fax).

Fathers' Resource Center, 430 Oak Grove Street, Suite B3, Minneapolis, MN 55403; frc@winternet.com.

National Fatherhood Initiative, 600 Eden Road, Building E, Lancaster, PA 17601; 717-581-8860; 717-581-8862 (fax).

NEWSLETTERS

At-Home Dad, Peter Baylies, 61 Brightwood Avenue, North Andover, MA 01845-1702.

Father Times, 430 Oak Grove Street, Suite 105, Minneapolis, MN 55403; 612-874-1509.

Fatherhood Today, National Fatherhood Initiative, 600 Eden Road, Building E, Lancaster, PA 17601.

Fathering Magazine, www.fathermag.com.

Full Time Dads: The Journal for Caregiving Fathers, P.O. Box 577, Cumberland Center, ME 04021; FullTDad@aol.com.